HAWAII

ANDREW W. LIND

Hawaii

THE LAST OF THE MAGIC ISLES

WITHDRAWN

Published for the
Institute of Race Relations, London
OXFORD UNIVERSITY PRESS
LONDON   NEW YORK   TORONTO
1969

Oxford University Press, Ely House, London W.1

GLASGOW NEW YORK TORONTO MELBOURNE WELLINGTON
CAPE TOWN SALISBURY IBADAN NAIROBI LUSAKA ADDIS ABABA
BOMBAY CALCUTTA MADRAS KARACHI LAHORE DACCA
KUALA LUMPUR SINGAPORE HONG KONG TOKYO

The Institute of Race Relations is an unofficial and non-political body, founded in England in 1958 to encourage and facilitate the study of the relations between races everywhere. The Institute is precluded by the Memorandum and Articles of its incorporation from expressing a corporate view. The opinions expressed in this work are those of the author.

Printed in Great Britain by
Billing & Sons Limited, Guildford and London

Contents

List of Tables

Preface

In a world as fraught with racial tensions as ours during the last half of the twentieth century, in which continents and nations, large and small, are embroiled in bitter conflict over issues centring on race, a volume on Hawaiian race relations may appear to have little relevance to the major issues of the day. Hawaii's infinitesimal size—a mere 6,400 square miles, most of it uninhabitable lava waste-land—and its geographic isolation by more than 2,000 miles from its nearest inhabited island or continental neighbours must raise doubts in some minds as to the possible insights to be derived from the Islands' limited experience. Most thoughtful observers may also be dubious regarding the applicability of any generalizations drawn from a supposedly simple island situation of half a million people to the intricate complexities of many millions and extending over centuries.

However, it is perhaps just because of its limited size and geographic inaccessibility in the vast Pacific, during most of the period since its discovery by Captain Cook in 1778, that Hawaii has greatly stimulated the imaginations and the pens of romanticists, from Robert Louis Stevenson and Mark Twain to William Allen White and James Michener. The result is that few areas in the world, considering their size and population, have figured more prominently in literature. From these writings a host of arresting but not too accurate characterizations of the Islands have emerged to capture the imaginations of many who have never seen Hawaii—phrases running the emotional gamut from 'the loveliest fleet of islands anchored in any ocean' to 'the golden man of the Pacific'.

Many, if not most, of these myths have centred upon the relationships among the numerous ethnic groups which have been attracted to the Islands, frequently by the golden magic which they were supposed to possess. According to some observers, the strange alchemy of the land is supposed to have transformed these thousands of impoverished peasants—who were drawn to Hawaii by the hope of winning a fortune for themselves alone or at most for their families—into altruists, dominated by *aloha*. Particularly in the area of race relations, there has appeared to be a need to examine some of these myths in a somewhat more realistic and objective atmosphere.

In an article written more than forty years ago, one of the Islands' many observers, an eminent American journalist, sought to portray the peculiar qualities of Hawaii's race relations and characterized Hawaii as 'The Last of the Magic Isles'. Many other writers, both before and since, have described Hawaii in terms which contain even greater elements of fantasy and make-believe without, however, recognizing the magic for what it is. This account of Hawaiian race relations is presented therefore under the title 'The Last of the Magic Isles', in the hope of dispelling some of the aura of mystery and wishful thinking which still surrounds so much of the thinking and writing relating to Hawaiian race relations.

I must hasten to disclaim any thought of providing an exhaustive analysis of so complex a subject as the relations among all the numerous racial groups of Hawaii. The notion that Hawaii in any of its major human relationships can be described in a few simple ideas, such as the aloha spirit, missionary altruism, or American democracy, is one of the most insidious and misleading of the myths with which the social scientist dealing with Hawaii has to contend. Rather, this volume has been conceived as an attempt to clear the atmosphere of some of the more prevalent myths and to suggest a basic framework of ideas within which a more comprehensive analysis of race relations may subsequently be made.

The first chapter, using the same title as that for the book, seeks to set the stage by reviewing the more commonly expressed but varied and even contrasting viewpoints of the Hawaiian racial scene, and closing with a summary of a conception of Island relations first presented by Romanzo Adams, to whose insights and sensitive appreciation of the Island setting this writer is gratefully indebted.

The second chapter, utilizing the concept of racial frontiers illuminated first by Robert E. Park, suggests the basic nature and a succession of typical situations out of which Hawaiian race relations have evolved. Instead of a simple, unified setting so commonly assumed, a series of sometimes conflicting, sometimes re-enforcing, and continually interacting systems of social relationships is presented.

The third chapter examines the way in which the conception of race has emerged in Hawaii as a by-product of the shifting frontier demands and traces the rise in social and economic status of the various racial groups as life emerges from one frontier to the other.

A fourth chapter gives special attention to the native Hawaiians as the one ethnic group whose experience has differed most markedly from the others by virtue of its retention of the qualities of a folk people in the midst of a society which has become largely industrialized. The Hawaiians are represented as caught between two conflicting and apparently irreconcilable sets of forces, the one to sustain a communally oriented and mutually re-enforcing mode of life and the other encouraging a competitive and individualistic approach.

A fifth and final chapter centres upon the more recent developments in Hawaiian race relations as they point to prospects for the future. Special attention is directed to the implications of mounting racial pride on the one hand and of prejudice on the other. Two tests of present and future trends in Hawaii's race relations are also introduced in this chapter, one of the limited experience of the American Negro in Hawaii and the other relating to the more general experience of mixed marriages and the birth of children of mixed racial parentage.

The author's observations and interpretations of data, which make up a considerable portion of this book, have been derived in large part from association and discussion with students and faculty colleagues at the University of Hawaii, upon whose insights and knowledge I have drawn as if they were my own. It would be quite impossible to list all of those to whom I am indebted for my education over the past forty years, nor would my tutors in many instances wish to be credited with some of the interpretations which I have attributed to their knowledge.

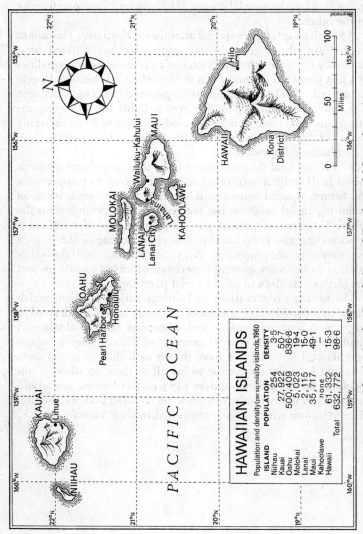

The Hawaiian Islands, showing Population and Density and Mountainous Areas

HAWAIIAN ISLANDS

Population and density (per sq. mile) by islands, 1960

ISLAND	POPULATION	DENSITY
Niihau	254	3·5
Kauai	27,922	50·7
Oahu	500,409	836·8
Molokai	5,023	19·4
Lanai	2,115	15·0
Maui	35,717	49·1
Kahoolawe	none	—
Hawaii	61,332	15·3
Total	632,772	98·6

1 | The Last of the Magic Isles

Scholars and laymen alike have long been prone to speak of Hawaii as if the phrase coined in 1926 by the visiting American journalist, William Allen White, were an accurate characterization of the Island social scene. The Kansas journalist, following a summer's experience as an observer of the Hawaiian social setting and as a participant in an international conference in Honolulu, evidently decided that he could best epitomize his observations of this mid-Pacific chain of islands under the title borrowed for this chapter, and the opening sentence carries the bold proposition that Hawaii is the one place in all the world where 'the so-called race problem is [not] acute', and where 'race injustices have disappeared because . . . race injustices are not in vogue'.[1]

Such a sweeping statement might readily be discounted as journalistic hyperbole except for the fact that so many other equally responsible observers have made comments in a similar vein. Visiting dignitaries—from prime ministers to film stars—when interviewed by the local press, seem impelled to make some reference to the peculiar inter-racial atmosphere of these islands as being different from and by implication superior to that of any other area of the earth. A former President of the United States, in his State of the Union Address, made special reference to the Islands as a 'unique example of a community that is a successful laboratory in human brotherhood', and serving therefore as 'a shining example of the American way to the entire earth'.[2]

[1] William Allen White, 'The Last of the Magic Isles', *Survey Graphic* (Vol. IX, no. 2, May 1926), p. 176.
[2] *Honolulu Star-Bulletin* (5 January 1956), p. 1.

The President was, of course, seeking first of all to mobilize legislative support for Hawaiian statehood, but he was at the same time reflecting a dominant conception of Hawaii as a human Utopia where America's professed ideals of freedom and equality without respect to 'race, color, or creed', had actually been consummated.

Even conservative social scientists repeat—regardless of whether they themselves accept or reject—the popular references to Hawaii as a 'polyracial paradise', 'the showcase of American democracy', and 'one of the most spectacular melting pots in the world'.[3] In one of the more recent college textbooks on ethnic minorities in America, the first sentence in a chapter on the peoples of Hawaii states that: 'Hawaii is a part of the United States where intergroup relations are unique.'[4] Others profess to find in the researches by seasoned Hawaiian scholars evidence of 'the almost complete absence of race prejudice and sustained social tolerance and cultural reciprocity'. In contrast with most other parts of the world where social cleavages frequently coincide with racial barriers, race in Hawaii is represented at most as something 'to be recognized but not to make a difference, as a basis of preferred loyalties, not of prescribed limitations'.[5]

This disposition to endow the Islands, and particularly their human and racial relationships, with unique and magical qualities has, of course, much more than mere academic or exotic significance.

DOUBTS AND SUSPICIONS

Quite understandably any system of social relationships which is presumed to be wholly unique, sooner or later also comes to be regarded with some suspicion, especially so if the system has been conceived in beneficent or Utopian terms. Unquestionably one of the prominent inducements which led the forty distinguished social scientists from various parts of the

[3] James W. Vander Zanden, *American Minority Relations* (New York, Ronald Press, 1966), p. 326.
[4] Charles F. Marden and Gladys Meyer, *Minorities in American Society* (New York, American Book Company, 1962), p. 352.
[5] Alaine Locke, *When Peoples Meet: A Study in Race and Culture Contacts* (New York, Progressive Education Association, 1942), p. 237.

world to convene in Honolulu in the summer of 1954 for the
Conference on Race Relations in World Perspective was to
ascertain for themselves what substance there might be to
Hawaii's reputation in the area of race relations. The published statement of one of these participants parallels the
private reactions of many more:

> One might be tempted to say that the racial situation in Hawaii
> is almost too good to be true. This was exactly the reaction of
> quite a number of participants at the recent Race Relations
> Conference in Honolulu. Some of them, and I must confess
> myself included, therefore did their best to find out the weak
> points in Hawaii's race relations.[6]

Needless to say, this observer found evidence to support his
scepticism, although obviously not to the point of disillusion-
ment:

> It is astonishing how quickly even strong prejudices die, once a
> person arrives in Hawaii. . . . If there is a group conflict in Hawaii
> it exists much more between generations than between races.[7]

Hawaii's reputation in race relations has not only been
questioned but also vigorously attacked as the poorly disguised creation by the exploiters of Hawaii's resources and
peoples to conceal their depredations. The more extreme of
these critics claim to have found in Hawaii's modern history
prior to World War II 'a story of imperialist plunder' in
which a 'high-powered ballyhoo . . . a synthesis of the popular conception of Hawaii, every capitalist "educational"
agency . . . is employed in the inculcation and perpetuation
of this fiction'.

> There are three main reasons why American imperialists paint
> a roseate view of Hawaii. First, it screens the slavery on the
> sugar and pineapple plantations. Second, it conceals military
> preparations for the next Pacific war. Third, tourists, readers,
> and movie fans pay millions for illusions of paradise.[8]

The contention of such interpreters of the Island scene is
that the popular version of Hawaiian race relations is not

[6] Walter Kolarz, 'The Melting Pot in the Pacific', *The Listener* (28 October
1954.)
[7] Ibid.
[8] Samuel Weinman, *Hawaii: A Story of Imperialist Plunder* (New York,
International Pamphlets, 1934), p. 3.

only false; it is diabolically false—a contrived scheme to entice innocent victims to their own destruction.

Another outlook on Hawaiian race relations is equally critical, not so much of the facts presented in the popular version as of the way in which they are interpreted. This point of view accepts more or less at face value the claims of interracial equality and freedom as expressed in the official pronouncements, but contends that the consequences of such a policy are socially deleterious. An admiral in the U.S. Navy, following an extended period of interracial tension in Honolulu, expressed convictions and attitudes which were shared by many of the newcomers to the Islands and especially those in the military services:

What is also disturbing is the intermixture of races that has been going on in the Hawaiian Islands for many years. Scientists have stated that these intermixtures tend to produce types of a lower moral and mental calibre than the pure-blooded types of each race, and this intermixture is increasing to an extent that will make each new generation of mixed bloods, with the continual introduction of a greater proportion of oriental blood, contain a majority of individuals of lower intellect and of increasing degeneracy.

The present system of self-government tends to increase the number of voters, and consequently of politicians and potential office holders, from amongst racial mixtures, bred for centuries with ideas of government, of social and living standards so diverse from our American ideals that the social and political conditions in these islands will have a tendency to drift further and further from such ideals. . . .

Present governmental control should be by men primarily of the Caucasian race, . . . by men who are not imbued too deeply with the peculiar atmosphere of the islands or with the predominance of inter-family connections; by men without preconceived ideas of the value and success of the melting-pot.[9]

Especially notable in the foregoing quotation is the expression of concern regarding 'the peculiar atmosphere of the islands' and the 'preconceived ideas of the value and success of the melting-pot'.

[9] Quoted in Seth W. Richardson, *Law Enforcement in the Territory of Hawaii* (Washington, U.S. Printing Office, 1932), pp. 198–9.

Statements as diametrically opposed to popular sentiment in the Islands as those quoted here would probably not have been stated in public, especially by a person in such a responsible position, except under the very strong provocation of an interracial crisis, such as the Massie incident (to be discussed later). Reactions comparable to those of the admiral, and sufficiently common to deserve passing attention, have, however, always been aroused among newcomers to the Islands and even, as expressed in private, among an undetermined minority of old-timers.

Other sceptics of the popular 'island-paradise' mythology are more restrained in their interpretation but manifest somewhat the same disposition to seek simplified explanations. There is, for example, the less extreme version of economic exploitation—that the original Western invaders of the Islands were indeed primarily concerned with the earning of maximum profits and did not hesitate to use the population, both native and immigrant labourers, to their own advantage. It developed, however, according to this version, that in their pursuit of self-interest, conditions were created which ultimately necessitated more humane treatment than characterized most other economic frontiers of the world. This viewpoint, of course, does not stress the peculiarity or uniqueness of Hawaii so much as the underlying similarity in the operation of universal economic laws, with any distinctions resulting only from the particular circumstances under which they work.

The prominent American journalist, Ray Stannard Baker, was one of the first among a series of 'muck-rakers' to give wide public expression to the now familiar thesis of economic dominance of race relations. Using the eye-catching but ambivalent caption of 'Wonderful Hawaii' for his three articles, Baker indicates his major theme in the opening paragraph:

Hawaii has been called, and justly called, the Paradise of the Pacific. But it is a paradise not only of natural beauties and wonder; it is also a paradise of modern industrial combination. In no part of the United States is a single industry so predominant as the sugar industry is in Hawaii, and nowhere else, perhaps, has the centralized control of property reached a state of greater perfection. Hawaii furnishes a vivid illustration of the way in which private business organization in its final stages of development permeates, influences, and controls the life of a country. Sugar is King in Hawaii to a far greater extent than cotton was in the Old South.[10]

Baker went on in his article to quote a still earlier 1905 report by the U.S. Commissioner of Labor to the effect that: 'Directly or indirectly all industries in Hawaii are ultimately dependent upon the sugar industry—the social, the economic, and the political structure of the islands is built upon a foundation of sugar.'

The European and American feudal aristocracy responsible for the building of the industry and the introduction of the various racial groups to supply its labour force, was represented as dominating the lives of the workers even to the most intimate details, including politics, education, and religion:

Every employee is directed at every turn and in nearly every detail of his life. I never knew a more complete nor more benevolent example of feudalism than this; and never more respectable and less democratic conditions.[11]

Such benevolence of the plantation aristocracy towards their non-white workers, unparallelled perhaps, as Baker contended, and a consequence of resident and missionary-oriented ownership and control, put ceilings on the social and economic status beyond which the immigrant workers could not expect to mount.

Fifty years later much the same thesis of an economic oligarchy controlling Hawaiian race relations during the first four decades of the present century was again widely publicized in the writings of another visitor to the Islands. Lawrence Fuchs, an American political scientist, however, carried his account of Hawaii's social history on into the post-war era when it seemed to him a new set of liberalizing political and educational forces was released:

[10] Ray Stannard Baker, 'Wonderful Hawaii: A World Experiment Station', *The American Magazine* (no. 11, November 1911), p. 28.
[11] Baker, op. cit. (no. 12, December 1911), p. 213.

In Hawaii, the socially superior—the *kamaaina haole* [old-timer of West European ancestry] controlled not only the normal points of the political process, but labour and wealth in the Islands as well. . . . Even by American, rather than colonial, standards, the oligarchy in Hawaii was more beneficent and charitable than were controlling groups in most rural areas on the mainland or many captains of industry and finance in Chicago, New York, and Pittsburgh. If most of the men who ran Hawaii during the 1920s and '30s believed in the racial supremacy of Caucasians and opposed labor unions, they were not different from the vast majority of their counterparts on the mainland. . . . No community of comparable size on the mainland was controlled so completely by so few individuals for so long.[12]

The potentials for change already existed in Hawaii's public-school system and the guarantee by Congress of the right of every American citizen to vote. . . . But war gave the greatest impetus to change. The schools were crucibles of democracy; World War II was its catalyst. . . . Democracy erupted, with its tensions and strains, but with opportunities too.[13]

James Michener, author of the widely read novel, *Hawaii*, from which the equally popular film of the same title was drawn, credits Fuchs with providing the basis for understanding where he 'might have gone wrong in some of [his] interpretations and where [he] fell short of writing the detailed truth'.

RACIAL UNORTHODOXY

Without minimizing the significance of the economic factors operating in Hawaii's race relations, the observers with longer and wider experience in the Islands have been less disposed to rely exclusively on the above or any other interpretation of what has transpired. Hawaii's pioneer sociologist, Romanzo Adams, has provided some of the most penetrating insights as to what is distinctive about the race relations of the Islands in a paper published under the title *The Unorthodox Race Doctrines of Hawaii*. Adams' major thesis was that owing to the peculiar circumstances under which

---

[12] Lawrence Fuchs, *Hawaii Pono: A Social History* (New York, Harcourt, Brace and World, 1961), p. 152.
[13] Ibid., p. 262.

the initial contact between the native Polynesians and the European explorers occurred, relationships between them developed from the outset on the basis of equality and mutual respect. This, he pointed out, was contrary to the experience in most other parts of the world where the confrontation of two or more racial groups has commonly resulted in relationships of superiority and inferiority in power and privilege between one group and the others.

Both indigenes and invaders possessed certain advantages which the others lacked and desired, and in the absence of any pronounced political or military superiority of either side, the resulting relationship tended to be one of mutual acceptance and tolerance, at the very least. Once the contacts between Caucasians and natives had become firmly established in custom and tradition on an equalitarian basis, a corresponding set of re-enforcing moral sanctions and doctrines (rationalizations to justify their code) likewise came into being. Thus the visitor to Hawaii, even though he comes thoroughly indoctrinated with the ethnocentric and discriminatory attitudes towards race in other areas, encounters the Island code requiring treatment of respect across racial lines, and although conformity may be grudging at the outset, his continued experience in a community where inter-racial respect is taken for granted tends eventually to his adoption of the Island code. Adams was well aware that even long-term residents (*kamaainas*) might hold and express in private racial attitudes contrary to the Island code but it was his contention that these 'cannot be openly avowed, . . . expressed in slogans . . . influence the civil law or the social code' and hence constitute at best a 'rear-guard action to cover a retreat'.

In short, the race mores of Hawaii are, or tend to be, the mores of race equality and the doctrines are, therefore, unorthodox from the standpoint of white people.[14]

Stress upon the 'mores of equality' as the dominant theme in Hawaiian race relations can readily be interpreted as

[14] Romanzo Adams, 'The Unorthodox Race Doctrine of Hawaii', in E. B. Reuter (ed.), *Race and Culture Contacts* (New York, McGraw-Hill, 1934), p. 148.

merely another version of the simplified 'Magic Isles' approach, and if this were the only formulation of the Hawaiian racial scene, the charge would be fully justified. For example, many of the university students of Island race relations whose background reading included Adams' essay have obviously sympathized with the South African social psychologist who exclaimed in exasperation at a conference on race relations in Honolulu that: 'The only real difference between race relations in South Africa and in Hawaii is that where I come from we openly admit that we discriminate on the basis of race, whereas your hypocritical code won't permit you to admit that you do.' The important and distinctive fact about Hawaiian race relations is, of course, the existence of a code of equalitarian relations which is deeply rooted in and has developed out of customary conduct of a similar nature, and the code does then exercise a coercive influence upon all who might be disposed to violate it. This point of view does not imply that the code is always adhered to or that competing patterns of conduct may not also exist.

Although the physiographic differences among the eight major islands of the Hawaiian archipelago, spread as they are over an oceanic arc 400 miles long, are frequently suggested as possibly contributing to deviations from Hawaii's traditional code of race relations, scholars have not taken this hypothesis very seriously. On the contrary, one prominent psychologist has referred—whether facetiously or not is difficult to tell—to the greater 'human plasticity' and the tolerance in race relations among both indigenes and immigrants as a consequence of the mild, sub-tropical environment throughout the Islands. He contends that the pleasant climate and ease of living in Hawaii have had a mellowing influence on the temperament of natives and immigrants alike, making the Hawaiians more 'malleable . . . and decidedly less belligerent' than their Maori first cousins and possibly supplanting the bigotry and greed among *Haole* (foreign) missionaries and traders by 'good humor, tolerance, and generous living'.[15]

---

[15] Stanley Porteus, *And Blow Not the Trumpet* (Palo Alto, Pacific Books, 1947), pp. 26–39.

II | Frontiers of Race Relations

The more widely accepted theory among social scientists is that the Island code of racial equality and the customary conduct which is consistent with that code are indeed largely a consequence of factors in the environment—but of factors which are social and institutional rather than physical or climatic. Robert E. Park, perhaps the foremost pioneer in the study of race and race relations in America and the Pacific basin and an observer in Hawaii for somewhat more than a year, introduced the term 'frontier' as a central concept in race relations, referring to the social situations in time and space where peoples of diverse cultures and prior residence are brought together and intermingle. In one of his most widely quoted articles, incorporating for the first time the terms racial frontier and race relations cycle, Park found in the Hawaiian experience an apt illustration of both these conceptions:

In the Hawaiian Islands, where all the races of the Pacific meet and mingle on more liberal terms than they do elsewhere, the native races are disappearing and new peoples are coming into existence. Races and cultures die—it has always been so—but civilization lives on.[1]

A few years later, Park discovered in the stimulating, multicultural atmosphere of Hawaii the basis for extending the conception of racial frontiers to a world-wide setting,[2] and in so doing, he laid some of the groundwork for the Confer-

[1] Robert E. Park, 'Our Racial Frontier on the Pacific', *Survey Graphic: East by West—Our Windows on the Pacific* (Vol. IX, no. 2, May 1926), p. 196.
[2] Robert E. Park, 'Race Relations and Certain Frontiers', in E. B. Reuter (ed.), *Race and Culture Contacts* (New York, McGraw-Hill, 1934), pp. 57–85.

ence on Race Relations in World Perspective which finally took place in Honolulu in 1954. This same conception provides now the basis for shifting to a more realistic and analytical basis the further consideration of race relations in Hawaii, which thus far has been in broadly theoretical, speculative, and at times oversimplified terms.

In race relations, as in so many other areas of human interaction, the nature of the initial contacts assumes a critical significance usually extending far beyond the lifetime of the persons originally involved. Hawaii's physical location, so far off the routes on which land-hungry monarchs had sent their explorers in search of spoils during the period of Western expansion of the eighteenth and nineteenth centuries, gave to these Islands a special immunity from the economic and political exploitation to which so many other areas were subjected. It was pure accident that Hawaii's discovery by the Western world should have occurred as a part of a voyage, not of military conquest but of an attempt to find a north-west passage from the Pacific to the Atlantic, and no external political power found it expedient to lay claim to the Islands by show of military force even after news of the 1778 discovery became known in the West.

The additional circumstances of Hawaii's relatively small size in the midst of such vast oceanic wastes, its apparent lack of natural resources, and its being most distant from strategic centres and routes of importance to the Western nations then engaged in colonial expansion, constituted further safeguards from outside military seizure and subjugation to which other areas in the Pacific were subjected. Thus, apart from sporadic demonstrations by European or American gunboats to enforce some special demands by Western traders, planters, or missionaries in the Islands, Hawaii escaped for well over a century after its discovery the political dependency which overtook most of its island neighbours much earlier.

THE TRADING FRONTIER

One of the major elements in Hawaii's peculiar pattern of race relations is a consequence of the fact that trade preceded rather than followed the flag, and trade, when it is unaccompanied by additional pressures, is essentially an equalitarian type of relationship. The parties engaged in trade do so presumably in the hopes of deriving maximum advantage from the transaction and each is equally free to sever the relationship if it appears that his interests are not being adequately served. From the very first day (18 January 1778) of direct contact between Captain Cook and the members of his crew with the natives on the island of Kauai the dominant concern of all the Haole visitors for the next forty years was in securing supplies of fresh fruit, vegetables, meat, water, and fuel in exchange for such of their own wares as the Hawaiians might be desirous of obtaining. The account in Cook's journal of his initial dealings with the Hawaiians reflects the impersonal, calculating, but also equalitarian nature of the interaction throughout this period:

I tied some brass medals to a rope, and gave them to those in one of the canoes, who, in return, tied some small mackerel to the rope, as an equivalent. This was repeated; and some small nails, or bits of iron, which they valued more than any other article, were given them. For these they exchanged more fish and a sweet potato; a sure sign that they had some notion of bartering; or at least of returning one present for another. . . . Others came off as we proceeded along the coast, bringing with them roasting pigs and some very fine potatoes, which they exchanged, as the others had done, for whatever we offered them. Several small pigs were purchased for a sixpenny nail so that we again found ourselves in a land of plenty.[3]

The traders who followed the explorers as the principal Western visitors to Hawaii, it is true, can hardly be credited with altruism in their relations with the natives. They obviously derived as much satisfaction as did Captain Cook from the purchase of native goods at low prices, and it is to be assumed that most of the traders took whatever advantage they could of the inexperience and ignorance of the Hawaiians. Certainly in the light of Western knowledge, the natives of these islands, no less than in other parts of the Pacific, were frequently victimized and cheated during the

[3] James Cook, *A Voyage to the Pacific Ocean* (London, W. and H. Strahan, 1784), Vol. II, pp. 191–2.

early years of contact, and Hawaiian hospitality was often abused. By its very nature, however, trade is a type of out-group relationship which requires the willing participation of both parties, and there is evidence that at least some of the natives learned to play the game as effectively as the foreigners. Moreover, in the absence of any foreign military power to enforce extortionate demands, any Western trader who expected to continue in business in Hawaii could not afford to develop a reputation as a scoundrel and a cheat. There were instances of trading operations degenerating into physical conflict, but these were the exceptions to the general rule of peaceful and mutually acceptable relations.

Other foreign visitors to the Islands during this initial period of contact—adventurers and deserting sailors—as well as the traders, were the guests, so to speak, in a foreign land, and any expectation of their continued acceptance in the Islands was clearly contingent upon corresponding attitudes of tolerance and respect towards the native people and their culture. Those who sought continuing and more inti-mate association with the Hawaiians as husbands or friends became obligated not only to tolerate but also to adopt for themselves some of the customs and values of the Islanders, and inevitably many 'went native' to a greater or lesser degree.

The development of reciprocal attitudes among the Hawaiians towards the visitors and their culture was equally evident and understandable. Captain Cook and the other early explorers were very much impressed with the enthu-siasm shown by the Hawaiians towards the material posses-sions of the Haoles, and especially of their iron:

In the course of my several voyages, I never met with the natives of any place so much astonished as these people were upon entering a ship. Their eyes were continually flying from object to object; the wildness of their looks and gestures fully expressing their entire ignorance about everything they saw. . . . They seemed only to understand that it [iron] was a substance much better adapted to the purposes of cutting, or of boring holes, than anything in their own country. They asked for it by the name of *hamaite* . . . which they wished might be very large.[4]

[4] Cook, op. cit., p. 233.

The eagerness with which the Hawaiians sought Western tools and artefacts, whose superiority to their own was readily evident, explains in part their willingness to tolerate at least some of the cultural values of the West which differed markedly from their own. There was much, for example, in the grasping, individualistic, and competitive nature of the trading relationships introduced by Caucasians which must have impressed the natives as being in sharp opposition to the communally shared and permissive mode of life within their own community. The outgoing generosity inherent in Hawaiian culture (see Chapter IV) was in itself a factor contributing to the acceptance of contrary dispositions among the Haoles, particularly in so far as the material advantages to be derived from and through the calculating foreigners were so obvious.

The Christian missionary movement, introduced to Hawaii in 1820, is sometimes credited with responsibility for the cordiality which exists in Island race relations. The part which the small group of New England Protestant missionaries performed in the total social, political, and economic life of the Islands was so impressive that it is assumed that this dominant influence must also have extended to race relations. The Christian gospel of the brotherhood of man under the fatherhood of God obviously had its implications in the relations between the missionaries and the natives; there would have been no adequate justification for the mission itself without the parallel assumption that the Hawaiians were potentially worthy of the efforts on their behalf. The charge given to the first mission prior to its departure from Boston in 1819, although somewhat vague in its reference to the Hawaiian people, was quite explicit in its definition of the civilizing function of the mission to them:

You are to aim at nothing short of covering those islands with fruitful fields and pleasant dwellings, and schools and churches; of raising up the whole people to an elevated state of Christian civilization. . . . To make them acquainted with letters; to give them the Bible with skill to read it; to turn them from their barbarous courses and habits; to introduce and get into extended operation and influence among them, the arts, institutions, and usages of civilized life and society; above all, to convert them from their idolatries and superstitions and vices, to the living and redeeming God; . . . to effect all this must be the work of an invincible and indefectible spirit of benevolence.[5]

The preoccupation of the missionaries with the absolute superiority of their own set of moral values and the associated customs and practices led, of course, to bitter condemnation of native culture, which appeared at times to be directed against those who were the carriers of that culture, as well:

We need not tell you that a nation like this, so sunk in indolence, ignorance, and mental imbecility, and so besotted in sin, cannot be elevated to enterprise, to intelligence, and moral greatness in a day. . . . The work of training up to refinement and to habits of physical, intellectual, and moral energy, a people so blinded, so ruined by the god of this world as the Sandwich Islanders, is not like the putting up of a shepherd's tent. It is the work of years, and of generations. . . . We who are now in this field . . . have begun the work of civilizing a savage nation; and, by the blessing of God, we have seen its steady advancement in spite of the opposition of earth and hell.[6]

Despite the avowed optimism in the ultimate triumph of the gospel over the pagan ways of the Hawaiians, the missionaries felt compelled to segregate their own children from possible contamination through close association with the natives and the partially segregated pattern of education which prevailed in Hawaii during much of the nineteenth and the early twentieth centuries can be traced to the determination to root out the 'evils' of Hawaiian culture.

One commonly overlooked, yet critical, factor in the part which the missionaries played in Hawaii's developing race relations was that, like the traders, their right to live and their physical well-being in the Islands were so largely dependent upon the goodwill of the native rulers. In Hawaii, as well as in other parts of the Pacific, it was clearly expedient and it seemed 'right' for the missionaries to address their

[5] Quoted in Ralph Kuykendall, *The Hawaiian Kingdom, 1778–1854* (Honolulu, University of Hawaii, 1938), p. 101.
[6] 'Extracts from the General Letter of the Mission', *Missionary Herald* (Vol. XXXIII, July 1837), pp. 276–7.

initial efforts, especially in education, towards the adult natives of noble rank, thus accelerating by the influence of upper-class example the 'civilizing' objectives of the missionaries. It was only natural that the missionaries should in a number of instances become the special confidants and advisers to the native rulers and chiefs, and as early as 1938 one of them severed his connections with the mission to become adviser to the King on matters relating to the State. Subsequently other members of the mission served on the King's cabinet, as Ministers of Foreign Affairs, Finance, Interior, and Public Instruction, and as Attorney-General. Not only were the early enacted laws and the first constitution of the Hawaiian kingdom largely inspired and written by Protestant missionaries, but a number of them were highly instrumental in preserving native rule when independence was threatened by belligerent foreign powers.

Despite the growing foreign influence in Hawaii's economic and political affairs, a Hawaiian monarch was on the throne throughout all but the last decade of the nineteenth century, and however much the foreigners might have entertained private doubts as to the capacity of the native rulers and might even have sought to displace them, such attitudes and efforts could not be revealed in public. On the contrary, as Adams insisted, the foreigners tended to bring their private dispositions into harmony with the recognized expedient behaviour. Both the traders and the missionaries, the two dominant groups of foreigners during the first half of the previous century, were by the nature of their vocations dependent on the natives, whether for profits or for souls, and the deferential and respectful posture towards the out-group which was demanded in their daily affairs tended eventually to become internalized as part of a code of equalitarian race relations.

THE PLANTATION FRONTIER

By the middle of the nineteenth century a new set of demographic and economic forces had come into play in Hawaii, out of which the first major threat to the permissive and equalitarian pattern of race relations, namely the plantation, likewise emerged. In very much the same way as in most of the other island areas of the Pacific, Hawaii experienced soon after discovery by the West a devastating loss in population through the introduction of diseases to which the indigenes had no natural immunity. The decline in the number of Hawaiians within fifty years from an estimated 300,000 in 1778 to less than half (134,750) in 1823 had the effect, among others, of releasing somewhat more than a similar proportion of the arable land area for new and potentially more advanced uses in the production of plantation crops. The downward trend continued throughout the remainder of the century, reducing the Hawaiian population in 1853 to less than a quarter and by the end of the century to little more than one-tenth of their pre-European numbers. A basic requirement of the plantation for extensive areas of land suitable for the cultivation of staple crops was thus ironically provided in Hawaii through the wasting away of the native population.

It was, however, in meeting the demands for the other major requirement of the plantation—a plentiful supply of inexpensive and tractable labour—that a new frontier in race relations was brought into being and the existing code was at least temporarily threatened. It might be assumed that the native Hawaiians, diminishing in numbers though they were, would have been able to supply the necessary labour, at least during the early stages of plantation development. In Hawaii, as in other plantation frontiers around the Pacific, the diminished native population had access to sufficient land and other resources to satisfy their simple standard of living by a few hours of toil in the taro patches during the cool morning or evening hours, with the rest of the day free for more pleasurable activities, such as fishing, swimming, or sleeping. There were no sound reasons for obligating themselves to work steadily, day in and out from sunrise to sunset, simply to satisfy a foreign taskmaster.

Under such circumstances, the Western plantation promoter must either resort to the enslavement of the native population, a practice with which the plantation has frequently been associated in other parts of the world, or he must import workers from areas where the supply is plentiful. Because Hawaii was an independent native kingdom, the foreign planters obviously could not subject the Islanders to slavery, and they were therefore compelled to recruit labourers from areas of 'closed resources' where labour was in over-supply and the means of securing a livelihood were scarce. Thus, beginning in 1852 with the arrival of 293 Chinese under contract to work for five years at a wage of $36 per annum in addition to passage, food, clothing, and housing, a flow of more than 400,000 labourers was recruited from widely separated regions around the world to man the sugar plantations of Hawaii. The regions most heavily tapped for labour over the succeeding century were, in order of the numbers involved, Japan; the Philippines; China; the Azores and Madeira Islands of Portugal; Spain; Korea; Puerto Rico; other islands of the Pacific; Russia; Germany; Norway; Manchuria; the southern states of the U.S.; and Italy. The entire demand for labourers on the plantations in Hawaii could easily have been supplied more cheaply from a single region relatively close at hand, such as South China, but to reduce the dangers of possible labour disturbances and to exercise better control the planters divided the workers among sharply contrasted ethnic stocks and maintained distinct physical and social barriers among them.

Having invested so much in procuring their labour supply, it is not surprising that the planters should seek to conserve by every possible means, including force, what had cost them so dearly. In lieu of slavery, so commonly utilized on plantation frontiers elsewhere but politically unfeasible in Hawaii, a substitute in the form of contract labour, providing penalties, including imprisonment, for desertion or refusal to obey orders, was invoked in Hawaii throughout the second half of the nineteenth century. Thus, on those portions of the Islands where plantation agriculture was economically feasible, a highly stratified order of life came into being with a small proprietary and managing group of Europeans or Americans socially isolated from, but at the same time dominating, the activities and life of a large mass of unskilled workers, commonly defined as separate races.

As a frontier settlement, the plantation was compelled to provide all the necessities of life for its immigrant workers, and the planter proprietor or manager became the virtual lord of an independent domain, accountable only in a limited sense to the owners and regularly constituted political authorities. The planter not only had to feed, clothe, house, and doctor his workers, he also found it expedient to establish rules for their conduct—when they should rise in the morning and go to bed at night, where they might go and what they might do with their leisure time. This arrogation by the planter or his immediate subordinates of the right to govern the conduct of persons of other cultural traditions throughout all twenty-four hours of every day frequently became extremely oppressive, especially as it extended over a period of years, and accentuated the resentment of the immigrants towards an institution and a way of life that offered far less than they had been led to expect when they first came to Hawaii. The maintenance of segregated camps for the various ethnic groups was an effective device both for keeping the workers in their places and for providing some cultural warmth and congeniality among them through the use of the language and the religious moral traditions of the home land, and this practice was continued well into the present century. Especially in the more remote sections of the Islands where the influence of the Hawaiian Government was slight, the plantation bosses frequently succumbed to the temptation to use force in controlling the workers, and stories of the *Haole luna* (white foreman) on horseback with his blacksnake whip continued well into the present century and long after the practice of flogging had ceased.

An objective comparison of the labour controls on the plantations of Hawaii, as compared with those of most other parts of the world at a corresponding stage of development, indicates that the workers in the Islands fared rather better than most—at least in the sense that there was less physical brutality and more genuine interest in the workers as human beings rather than merely as instruments of production. The children and grandchildren of immigrant labourers, it is true, still repeat the accounts they have heard of the use by plantation lunas of the club and the whip, and of labourers being driven from the sick-bed to work in the fields, but such abuses were the acts of desperation and the conditions which encouraged them have long since disappeared.

The plantation situation in Hawaii in which ownership and management has been from the outset by permanent Island residents has made possible the highly effective and centralized labour control by the so-called 'Oligarchy'. The corporations known as the Big Five, commonly credited by many observers with monopoly control over Island economic, political, and social affairs during the first third of the present century, developed originally as the business agents for the sugar plantations. The Big Five, with their interlocking directorate in Honolulu which includes also the Hawaiian Sugar Planters Association, were able to manage the various immigrant labour groups very much to their own advantage and so limit the hazards of labour organizations and strikes. A notable aspect of the control exercised by the planters and the Big Five in Hawaii, as compared with other plantation frontiers, was not only its greater centralized efficiency, but also the presence of a greater emphasis upon human welfare, which is objectively characterized as follows in a 1915 U.S. Department of Labor report:

> The plantation interests form a benevolent industrial oligarchy. The relations existing between the plantation manager and his laborers are semifeudal. Laborers and their families on the sugar plantations, for the most part living in isolated village communities, are accustomed to regard the plantation manager as an earthly providence whose paternal business is to supply them with certain utilities and disutilities with or without their advice and consent. Other industries are either unable or both unable and unwilling to do as much for their laborers in the way of medical, nursing, and hospital treatment, water supply, camp and house sanitation, amusements, and the like.[7]

Probably hard-headed business sense, rather than the religious motives sometimes attributed to the Island planters, accounted for most of this programme. The humane and

[7] *Labor Conditions in Hawaii, Fifth Annual Report of the Commissioner of Labor on Hawaii* (Document no. 432, 64th Congress, Washington, 1916), pp. 66–7.

generally intelligent type of treatment accorded Hawaiian plantation employees is also a consequence of the fact that the owners and managers of the plantations have so largely continued to live in the Islands and have been responsive to local public opinion and to the missionary tradition.

Thus, while the institutional nature and requirements of the plantation must be credited with the introduction to Hawaii of most of the groups known here as races, the very conception of race as a divisive category is largely a function of the plantation system. Prior to the plantation era, the only important distinction with any clear resemblance to race observed in Hawaii was between the natives and the foreigners and this distinction was primarily cultural and did not necessarily imply a difference in status or class. For example, in the early official censuses before the arrival of large plantation labour groups, the Chinese were included in the growing category of foreigners, and it was not until after a considerable number had been brought in as plantation and domestic workers with a status inferior to that of the Haoles that the Chinese came to stand out as a separate racial group and were so recognized in the census of 1866. Similarly the Portuguese, Spanish, and Norwegian immigrants did not differ markedly in religion or cultural heritage from their plantation overlords, but were classified as distinct racial groups in the official census as long as their place within the economy of Hawaii was at the inferior level of plantation labour.

The plantations of Hawaii had reached the zenith of their economic and political power, and thus indirectly, of their influence on race relations, well within the first third of the nineteenth century. The proportion of Hawaii's gainfully employed population engaged in agriculture, of whom the overwhelming majority were plantation workers, had been declining steadily after 1870—from 86 per cent in 1872 to 62 per cent in 1900 and to 40 per cent in 1930. Plantation production, however, continued to expand throughout the first three decades of the twentieth century, and so likewise did the population deriving their income from and living under the shadow of the plantation. In the early 1930s

C

roughly one-half of the entire population of Hawaii were either sugar and pineapple plantation workers or their dependants. During the second third of the twentieth century the dominance of the plantation as affecting the total life of the Islands, including its race relations, was eclipsed by that of competing sources of livelihood, notably the military establishment and tourism. The striking decline in the number of employees on the sugar plantations from a peak of 51,427 in 1932 to 10,960[8] in 1962 affords a somewhat exaggerated indication of its waning institutional impact on Island race relations. Moreover, the plantation itself had changed markedly in the meantime. As the Island economy developed and its supply of labour expanded, the earlier necessity for the plantation to maintain such rigid controls along racial lines ceased to exist, residential and occupational segregation declined greatly, and advancement in status could occur on the basis of individual merit rather than of race.

POLITICAL FRONTIERS

Hawaii's political status as an autonomous nation for 120 years following discovery by the West is frequently represented in literature as a poorly disguised form of American colonialism with its racial discrimination piously concealed by a front of missionary concern for the ignorant natives. The comic-opera potential in Hawaii's mid-nineteenth century political experience, in which Hawaiian kings read lengthy speeches and promulgated ponderous documents of State, prepared wholly—or so it seemed—by Europeans and Americans, has been too great a temptation to be overlooked by foreign critics. No one familiar with Hawaiian history can fail to recognize the comic as well as the tragic aspects of the continuing interaction at the level of political manoeuvring between foreigners and natives, or to realize that laws

[8] Widespread mechanization and automation were the adjustments of management to the rising costs of labour brought on by federal legislation, unionization, and the mounting demands for labour in other fields. In spite of the phenomenal decline in the number of plantation workers after 1932 sugar production increased substantially during the same period of time.

were passed, Cabinet Ministers were appointed, treaties were signed with foreign powers, and even kings were seated in response to pressures emanating in large part from the Haoles. To conclude, however, from such evidence that Hawaii's show of political independence was only a form of puppetry in which the Hawaiians were the unwitting dupes of conniving foreigners is a gross oversimplification.

The very existence of foreigners, of people who did not belong to the Islands, created from their first appearance the possibility of racial tension. The essence of race relations is the presence in close juxtaposition of at least two groups—of those who belong and those who do not—although frequently it takes on an added dimension in that the outsiders possess some power that enables them to subjugate the insiders. By virtue of the peculiar circumstances existing in Hawaii, this latter development did not occur. There were, however, many tensions and even overt conflicts between the Hawaiian power structure and the foreigners, who sometimes were able to enlist the military arms of their home governments to support claims of varied types and frequently of questionable validity.

Captain Cook himself was involved and lost his life in the first of a long series of conflicts between the native Hawaiians and the foreigners. Despite the bloody nature of this first encounter, in which five British and a score of natives lost their lives, satisfactory working relationships were soon reestablished. In the absence of an exclusive or preponderant power on either side, the mutuality and equality associated with trade continued to dominate the relationships between indigene and foreigner for nearly a century. This is not to disregard the instances in which foreign traders and visiting admirals attempted to take the law into their own hands and sometimes succeeded temporarily. There was, for example, the infamous incident of 1790 in which a Captain Metcalfe of an American trading vessel, in retaliation for the theft of one of his small boats and the killing of one of his men, destroyed a Hawaiian village on Maui and subsequently massacred more than 100 natives whom he had encouraged to come out to his ship to engage in trade. By a curious combination of circumstances, a Hawaiian chief on another island who had been whipped by Captain Metcalfe for some petty offence, attained his revenge a few days later by seizing another small American ship, commanded by Metcalfe's 18-year-old son, and killing its crew. Five years later another incident, involving a sea captain widely known for his trade in guns and ammunition, resulted in the seizure by natives of two British trading ships and the killing of their commanders. But again peace was restored and trading went on as before.

In 1817 some Russians manoeuvred native chiefs into granting permission to establish for a short time a fort on the island of Kauai. In 1826 American traders persuaded the United States to send warships to collect unpaid debts and to enforce order on deserting sailors. French and British warships in 1837 and French warships again in 1839 threatened war unless Roman Catholic priests were allowed to propagate their religion. In 1843 a British naval captain demanded and secured the temporary cession of the Kingdom to Great Britain, but the independence of the Islands was subsequently restored. During this period various Western powers demanded and secured, under protest, special privileges for their citizens, and American commercial interests had agitated openly for annexation with the United States as early as 1840. By 1850 the threats of seizure of the Islands by filibustering elements from the American mainland were such that King Kamehameha had a treaty of annexation as an equal state of the United States drawn up for submission to Congress, but the necessary negotiations were never consummated. Foreign interests within Hawaii were never fully united, and although they continued to operate behind the scenes and to influence the policies of the Kingdom throughout the century, it was not until 1893 that even the trappings of native control were finally abandoned.

The revolution of 1893, resulting in the removal from the throne of Queen Liliuokalani, the last of the native Hawaiian monarchs, and the establishment of an independent republic, was largely in response to pressures from the American and other foreign commercial interests. Certainly the landing of troops in Honolulu from an American warship at the time of the 1893 Revolution was a factor contributing significantly, psychologically if in no other way, to the bloodless overthrow of the native monarchy. The final acceptance of territorial status under the United States in 1898 was commonly interpreted by the great mass of Hawaiians as the victory of the foreign plantation interests and a serious loss of self-esteem. Even the enactment of the Organic Act in 1900, which guaranteed equality before the law to all regardless of racial ancestry with, however, certain special economic advantages to Hawaiians and part-Hawaiians, could not wholly compensate for the affront to their pride.

The shift from independent political status under the Monarchy and the Republic to a dependent status as a Territory of the United States brought varied and in some instances conflicting consequences on Island race relations. The removal of earlier property qualifications, which only Haoles and a few others could meet, and the extension of the rights of citizenship to all persons born within the Islands had the effect in theory at least of equalizing among all racial groups the opportunities for participation in the political life and control of the community.

This broadening of the base and the democratizing of politics had extremely important consequences for a later generation, when the children of the large number of immigrant labourers, upon reaching maturity, could take advantage of these newly conferred privileges. The immediate changes were noted chiefly among the native Hawaiians and the immigrant labourers of Caucasian ancestry, such as the Portuguese, Germans, and Norwegians. The very much larger number of immigrants from the Orient—Chinese, Japanese, and Koreans—were by U.S. federal legislation automatically debarred from citizenship and hence from effective political participation. It was not until nearly a half century later, following World War II, when the majority of the immigrants from the Orient had either died or left the Islands, that this form of racial discrimination was removed by action of Congress.

One of the not wholly anticipated consequences of annexation was the influx of a considerable number of newcomers from the American mainland, many of whom were indoctrinated with conceptions of race which were foreign to Hawaii. For a short time after arrival, their alien point of view created a problem both for themselves and for the residents, but with the passage of time they tended either to absorb the 'unorthodox race doctrines of Hawaii', while subordinating their own earlier attitudes, or they left the Islands.

As a further consequence of Hawaii's losing its independence and becoming the western frontier of the United States, the Island mode of interaction across racial lines was subjected to further testing by the introduction of increasing numbers of outsiders, in this instance of military personnel. Unlike the many colonial frontiers where the invader's military might has established his dominance over the natives almost at the outset and where the right of physical force comes to symbolize the relationship between the races long afterwards, in Hawaii the purely military influence was relatively late in making its appearance.

American interest in Hawaii as a military outpost in the Pacific had obviously played a part in the execution of the 1876 Reciprocity Treaty between the two nations, in which Hawaiian sugar was allowed duty-free entry into the United States in return for American rights to develop Pearl Harbor. It was not, however, until thirty-two years later that work was actually begun on the construction of a naval station there, and although a small army garrison was established on the island of Oahu soon after the transfer of political control in 1898, another twenty years elapsed before any significant development occurred. According to the Hawaiian census of 1910, there were only 1,608 persons listed as 'soldiers, sailors, and marines', and even by 1920 this figure had only increased to 3,860, but by 1930 the number had increased to 15,862 and by 1940 to 29,057. The largest military population was reached during the period of World War II, when the military personnel outnumbered the total civilian population of the Islands. During the 1960s the military personnel in Hawaii has varied in number

between 50,000 and 60,000, and together with their dependants this element represented roughly one-seventh of the
total population in July 1967.

In general, however, the military influence on race relations has been operative within a restricted area of Island life.
On the military installations, situated almost wholly on the
island of Oahu, a type of racial segregation and stratification,
quite comparable to that on the early plantations, prevailed
until after the close of World War II. Prior to the 1948
Presidential Order calling for the gradual desegregation of
all military bases, these establishments had very much the
character of self-sufficient and independent States, where
traditions of a racial caste system could be maintained
without interference from the local community. In so far as
the military structure in the United States prior to 1948
sanctioned and enforced racial segregation and stratification,
there was little in the Hawaiian racial environment which
could be expected to counteract it within the military
establishment itself. Even after 1948 the dispositions to
discriminate racially in matters such as housing and recreation inevitably lingered on, especially when those in command had been disproportionately drawn from areas with
strong racial prejudices.

The relatively brief period of residence at any post per-
mitted under the American military system and the high
degree to which all possible needs may be satisfied on the
post provide little encouragement for members of the military
establishment to enter into serious communication with
members of the larger community in which they happen to
be stationed. Particularly in a community with as many
different and wholly unfamiliar ethnic groups as Hawaii, the
great mass of the military establishment recruited in continental United States shy away from unnecessary and potentially dangerous contacts with the Islanders. During the war
especially the term of opprobrium, 'gook', was widely used
by service men to refer to all local residents who seemed
markedly different or strange to them, and it has continued
to symbolize the social distance separating the majority of the
military personnel from most of the Island residents.

The few areas in which the large number of single men in the military forces commonly find the provisions on the base inadequate to meet their needs and where they consequently seek their satisfactions in the civilian community are, of course, those where out-group tensions are most likely to arise. For relief from the monotony and discipline of the military régime, many of the service personnel seek the stimulation and excitement of drugs, drink, and sex, and in all three, as outsiders, they compete at a considerable disadvantage with the local residents. The Madame-Butterfly type of experience has been familiar enough in every community with a sizeable military encampment close by, and in Hawaii there is a long tradition, extending well over a century, of the strangers from abroad who have wooed and won the favours of Island girls, only to leave them 'holding the bag'. Resentment towards the outsiders has become more or less chronic, therefore, on the part of Island young men who see in every service man from the mainland a potential rival to himself and a possible threat to his sister or girl friend. There is a long history of 'bad blood' between Islanders and men from the armed services in which broad racial identifications of 'gooks' *v.* 'shark bait' or 'white meat' have commonly been involved.

One of the most sensational, although not most typical, of these incidents was the so-called Massie affair which attracted world-wide attention in 1931–2. In this particular instance, the Haole wife of a junior naval officer was seized and assaulted, allegedly by a gang of local youths of mixed racial ancestries who were subsequently brought to trial but later discharged for lack of sufficient evidence. A considerable number of persons in the armed forces, especially in the Navy, became greatly incensed at the verdict—that the testimony of a white woman should carry no greater weight than the alibis of dark-skinned youths with police records—and some of the Navy personnel took the law into their own hands. One of the youthful defendants was kidnapped and severely beaten in an unsuccessful attempt to force him to confess his guilt, and the culminating episode in a series of tensions between military personnel and civilians was the admitted slaying of another of the defendants by Lt. Massie and two of his subordinates in the Navy for the supposed unpunished sex offence against Mrs. Massie. The sensational publicity regarding its 'white-coloured relations', which Hawaii had been receiving in the press of continental United States and Europe throughout the earlier phases of the Massie affair, was still further intensified when the world-famous attorney, Clarence Darrow, agreed to defend Lt. Massie and his two confederates in their trial for murder. A large part of the reporting to the mainland during the entire affair served to give the impression that no white woman was safe on Honolulu streets after dark because of the lawless gangs of Islanders of varied ancestries. It is safe to say that no other incident or series of incidents—not even the war—has so profoundly threatened the racial sensibilities and equanimity within Hawaii or the popular conceptions of them outside of Hawaii.

From a purely external viewpoint it would seem that Hawaii's traditional pattern of race relations would have been subjected to its most severe test by the identification of the Islands with the United States during World War II. As the war clouds were building up over the Pacific during the late 1930s and early 1940s, popular writers quite naturally focused attention on the presence within America's major fortress in the Pacific of a civilian population whose largest single ethnic group were the immigrants or the children of immigrants from the nation with which armed conflict seemed to be inevitable. Two widely publicized and supposedly responsible analyses of the Hawaiian scene shortly before the attack on Pearl Harbor[9] represented the presence of 138,000 Japanese as the source of major concern to the highly efficient military forces in 'their tight little Gibraltar'. There is ample evidence that many of the civilians, especially the recently arrived defence workers from the mainland, also conceived of the 37 per cent minority of Japanese as a dangerous 'enemy within'.

[9] 'Hawaii: Sugar-Coated Fort', *Fortune* (Vol. XXII, no. 2, August 1940), pp. 31–7, 78–81; Joseph Barber, Jr., *Hawaii: Restless Rampart* (New York, 1940).

The full account of what transpired on 7 December 1941 and subsequently, as affecting race relations, is much too involved to present in any detail. A summary statement prepared a few months after the Pearl Harbor attack touches some of the high points of that experience:

> The initial reaction of the overwhelming majority of all Island residents, regardless of racial ancestry or class, on December 7 was that 'It can't happen here'; and the ensuing sense of anger, dismay, and horror was wellnigh universal among the civilian population.
>
> It was to be expected that some of the revulsion and anger of the entire community at the events which took place in Hawaii on the morning of the Seventh should be directed toward those residents of the Islands who bore the visible and ineffaceable marks of kinship with the treacherous enemy. That no serious instances of mob attack upon Japanese residents of Hawaii occurred on the Seventh or thereafter is evidence of the effectiveness of prewar interracial solidarity, as well as of the military and police controls imposed. There were expressions of deep resentment but they were surprisingly few in number as compared with the expectations of many observers who were not familiar with the Island codes of conduct. . . .
>
> Instances of a similar [violent] sort were sufficiently frequent to provide adequate grounds for uneasiness among the Japanese. Nisei defense workers were ordered off the project at the point of a bayonet; medical attendants were prevented from doing their duties because they were of Japanese ancestry; trained civilians who responded to requests for guardsmen were refused posts while wholly inexperienced non-Japanese were accepted; maids who had given faithful service were summarily discharged.[10]

Immediately after the Pearl Harbor attack a host of rumours of wide-scale sabotage and fifth-column activity on the part of resident Japanese began to appear, emanating chiefly from among recent arrivals and later embellished in mainland newspapers and journals. The success of the attack —the accuracy of their knowledge of U.S. military locations and the speed and secrecy with which the attack was made—

[10] Andrew W. Lind, *The Japanese in Hawaii Under War Conditions* (New York, Institute of Pacific Relations, 1943), pp. 9–10.

all suggested the work of an enemy within, and who more likely than the resident Japanese? They were accused of sending messages to the enemy by signal lights, of poisoning the drinking water, of cutting arrows in the cane fields to direct Japanese pilots to military objectives, and of deliberately blocking traffic along strategic highways. Despite the testimony of the most reliable authorities, both civilian and military, that there were 'no known acts of sabotage, espionage or fifth-column activities committed by the Japanese in Hawaii either on or subsequent to December 7, 1941',[11] the rumours persisted in some areas until after the close of the war, and they doubtless contributed significantly to the increased distrust towards the Japanese among some Islanders and a greater tendency to withdraw on the part of many Japanese.

Paradoxically the imposition of martial law throughout Hawaii on 7 December, just a few hours after the initial attack, assisted substantially in the preservation of peaceful, if not friendly, relations across ethnic lines. One of the first regulations under martial law, it is true, imposed discriminatory prohibitions on all alien Japanese, 14 years of age and over—the possession or use of firearms, short-wave receiving sets, transmitting sets, signal devices, cameras, or maps of military installations, and of travel by air, change of residence or occupation or movement from place to place without military permission. At the same time, however, they were promised that:

So long as they shall conduct themselves in accordance with the law, they shall be undisturbed in the peaceful pursuit of their lives and occupations and be accorded the considerations due to all peaceful and law-abiding persons, except so far as restrictions may be necessary for their own protection and the safety of the United States. All citizens are enjoined to preserve the peace and to treat them with all such friendliness as may be compatible with loyalty and allegiance to the United States.[12]

Subsequent public assurances from the commanding

[11] See Andrew W. Lind, *Hawaii's Japanese* (Princeton, N.J., 1946), pp. 43–6.
[12] General Order No. 5, Military Governor of Hawaii, 8 December 1941. As quoted in Lind, op. cit., p. 69.

general by radio and press, of fair play and individual justice regardless of racial origin did much to preserve inter-ethnic stability and to encourage serious efforts to execute these principles in actual practice:

Hawaii has always been an American outpost of friendliness and goodwill and now has calmly accepted its responsibility as an American outpost of war. In accepting these responsibilities it is important that Hawaii prove that her traditional confidence in her cosmopolitan population is not misplaced.[13]

The adoption by the military authorities in Hawaii of a policy of humane and equalitarian treatment, consonant with the Island tradition, seems all the more noteworthy in view of the contrary policy of wholesale evacuation of Japanese on the Pacific Coast where the dangers of fifth-column activities were so slight by comparison. The officials responsible for the policies in Hawaii had fortunately lived long enough in the Islands to be influenced by its prevailing sentiments on race relations and thus to withstand the strong pressures from both civilian and military groups urging a more severe and uncompromising approach.

The actual execution of the policies, of course, did not always measure up to the professions. The treatment of the public in general under martial law, as carried out by individuals newly vested with autocratic powers, tended to be rigid and frequently inhumane, and persons of Japanese ancestry probably suffered most from such abuses. The order for the inactivation of the Japanese members of the Hawaii Territorial Guard on 21 January 1942 was an especially bitter blow to the pride of the entire Japanese community and appeared to offer incontrovertible evidence that, despite public protestations to the contrary, the citizens of Japanese ancestry were not trusted. The decision in June 1942 to transfer to continental United States all trained draftees of Japanese ancestry—approximately 2,000—as a separate combat unit appeared as further evidence of official distrust, but the extension of an offer to induct another 1,500 into

[13] Lt. General Delos C. Emmons, December 1941. As quoted in Lind, op. cit., p. 70.

the Army as volunteers did much to restore a sense of full acceptance.

The spectacular war record of the segregated units of Americans of Japanese ancestry served to remove the doubt that may once have existed as to their whole-hearted desire to be fully identified as Americans. The 442nd Regimental Combat Team, including the 100th Infantry Battalion, acquired a record as 'probably the most decorated unit in United States military history'. With the return of peace, the Island-born residents of Japanese ancestry had established their right to occupy positions of equality alongside all the other ethnic groups in Hawaii, and the earlier tendencies to accept unquestioningly a status subordinate to the Haoles especially, born in large part from earlier experience on the plantations, largely disappeared. This new sense of personal worth and dignity expressed itself in a variety of different ways—in a new disposition to expect equal treatment in industry, to participate in Island politics without reservation, and to speak out unhesitatingly on issues of community concern.

The major issue involving the status of the entire population of the Islands following World War II was whether Hawaii was to continue as a dependent Territory of the United States, with only limited political autonomy, or if it had developed sufficiently from its earlier semi-colonial status to merit full partnership with the other forty-eight States of the Union. Although the Territorial Legislature had gone through the motions of petitioning the U.S. Congress for statehood as early as 1903, it was not until after the Massie affair and the consequent threat of a commission form of government and the restrictions on the amount of sugar Hawaii could export to the mainland that serious efforts were made to secure passage of a statehood act. A series of Congressional hearings on the question of statehood, commencing in 1935, produced evidence of a growing dissatisfaction among Islanders of all ethnic backgrounds over the limitations to which they were subjected within the American commonwealth—their inability to elect their own Governor, to have voting representatives in Congress, and to participate in the election of the President of the nation, among other evidences of second-class citizenship. In a plebiscite conducted along with the general election in 1940—a distinctly unfavourable time considering the mounting international tension in the Pacific—the vote among Island citizens was more than two to one in favour of statehood.

Following the war, agitation for statehood increased further, particularly among those of Oriental ancestry who had felt most keenly the sense of being discriminated against in their relationships with continental United States. Additional hearings in Hawaii by members of Congress, commencing early in 1946, indicated that the greatly reduced but highly vocal opposition to statehood among Islanders came chiefly from among persons of Haole and Hawaiian ancestry. The limited opposition from among Haoles, in so far as it bore directly on race relations, came chiefly from persons, whether *malihini* (newcomer) or *kamaaina* (old-timer), who harboured prejudices towards the Oriental population, especially the Japanese, which only a critical issue such as statehood would bring them to express publicly. The underlying basis of most of the Hawaiian opposition was a fear that statehood would further undermine their position economically and politically in the Islands (see Chapter V).

The critical opposition, of course, came not from the Islands, but chiefly from the Representatives and Senators in Congress who looked with disfavour on the prospect of admission to a position of equality among the States of a region whose citizenry consisted so largely of non-whites. Although numerous other bases for opposing statehood were cited, such as Hawaii's non-contiguity and great distance from continental United States, the alleged stranglehold of Communist-dominated unions on the labour market, or a comparable control of the Island economy by the Big Five, it was the racial factor that figured most prominently among the small minority in Congress, chiefly from the southern states, who blocked passage of the Act until 12 March 1959.

It is not apparent that Hawaii's entrance into the Union as a fully accredited State has in and of itself produced any major shift in the relationships among the several ethnic groups. There has been a significant increase in the number of civilians from the U.S. Mainland, who have migrated to Hawaii since Statehood, amounting in recent years to somewhat more than 10,000 per year, but the fact that most of the newcomers are young, more than half of them under 24 years of age, according to a recent study, suggests that their racial outlook is susceptible to modification in the new environment. The resulting shift in the numerical balance of the races in the Islands to one in which the Caucasians now outrank the Japanese as the largest single ethnic group has not disturbed to any significant degree the existing pattern of permissive race relations.

TOURIST FRONTIERS

The most recent invasion of Hawaii, which promises now to outstrip all others in view of the numbers involved if not in the diversity of the ethnic backgrounds represented and its impact on Island race relations, is of tourists in search of diversion and recreation. The appeal of strange and distant places has doubtless figured prominently in the motivation of most of the visitors to Hawaii, from the sailors who accompanied Captain Cook on his voyage of discovery to the hordes of tourists who swarm on the mammoth jetliners and ocean-going hotels which visit the Islands today. To a greater or lesser degree, even the traders, missionaries and plantation workers, and the soldiers, sailors and marines of a later day have felt the pull of possible adventure in a new environment. There is, however, an added institutionalized character to the tourist industry of the present generation which bears more directly on the concerns of race and race relations.

Mark Twain was probably the first of a series of American writers of fiction to glamourize the Islands for the benefit of the tourist industry. Probably no aphorism has been more frequently quoted to induce strangers to 'see for themselves' than his sweetly sentimental references to 'the loveliest fleet of islands that lie anchored in any ocean', with its 'summer seas flashing in the sun', and 'plumy palms drowsing by the shore'. The conditions for the effective exploitation of Mark

Twain's enthusiastic description of the Islands in the cause of tourism, however, did not develop for more than half a century after he wrote, and by this time a new school of professional travel writers had begun to appear with a greater emphasis on the more tangible inducements which Hawaii had to offer.

The striking rise in family incomes in the United States, together with a corresponding technical advancement and consequently lowered costs in air transport are the two principal factors contributing to the phenomenal expansion in the number of tourist visitors to Hawaii in the period following World War II—from 15,000 in 1946 to over one million in the year 1967, with the prospect of more than two million in the year 1975. The sheer numbers involved, far exceeding the resident population at present, would seem to offer the possibility of transforming the equality of race relations within the Islands in a short space of time, and there are those observers who predict that this will occur. An examination of what has happened during the more than twenty years since the war indicates clearly that significant changes have occurred but not always in the direction or to the degree that is commonly expected.

Like all the other visitors to the Islands, the tourists bring with them whatever racial doctrines and moral sentiments they had developed at home. What differentiates the tourists from all other visitors, however, is the fact that they are at the same time seeking to escape—perhaps from boredom, as well as from some of the obligations and expectations by which they are restrained at home. They are, for a brief period of days, weeks, or months, leaving behind their usual concerns and responsibilities, including those of preserving the racial definitions and prejudices of the home community. It might be said that they are in pursuit of new experiences, even those which would normally be shocking, so as to be able to command the attention and interest of their friends when they return home. One of the paradoxical aspects of tourism is that the individuals who are most careful to preserve the conventionally defined distances between themselves and other ethnic or racial groups at home frequently become most enamoured with persons of these same or other out-groups in the permissive atmosphere of Hawaii. Because the tourist experience is transitory and socially segmental, involving chiefly the adventure-loving or thrill-seeking aspects of personality and not the whole person, it is always susceptible of exploitation, and this is even more pronounced when it cuts across cultural and racial barriers.

The institutionalized structure which develops to deal with this type of situation is necessarily characterized by a certain artificiality and insincerity. The Islanders who derive their livelihood by the service they render to the tourists tend inevitably to cater to the desires of their guests or what is believed to be those desires. The promoters of the tourist industry in Hawaii, especially the large aeroplane and steamship lines, commonly present in their national advertising a picture of Hawaii in terms of happy, care-free, musical, lei-bedecked and loving Polynesians against a backdrop of the summer seas, plumy palms, and woodland solitudes which Mark Twain popularized a century ago. Much of the tourist literature also depicts both the physical and the social setting in romanticized and sentimental language, with major emphasis upon the native Hawaiians as a simple, childlike, lovable and uninhibited people.

The use which is made by the tourist promoters of the Hawaiian term *aloha*, commonly translated as love or affection, illustrates the possible abuse which may occur when a relationship which is essentially commercial and utilitarian is represented as one of intimate and friendly concern. The aloha spirit of freely giving for the pleasure of giving without thought of return, is peculiarly identified with the ancient Hawaiian folk culture in which property rights were to a considerable degree communally held and therefore readily shared. Under the individualistic and competitive relationships which exist in today's economy, however, such dispositions naturally tend to atrophy, and consequently the gap between profession and practice inevitably widens. Quite obviously those who would adhere strictly to the principle of aloha in their economic relations, as expressed in the familiar Hawaiian phrase, 'Come in, the house is yours', must

D

have some assurance that others will conduct themselves on a similar basis. The native Hawaiians and part-Hawaiians, whose conduct is most widely governed by such traditional dispositions of open hospitality, are, of course, most likely to be victimized by a system in which aloha is more of a slogan than a reciprocally operating force. The growing realization that their generosity and hospitality frequently fails to be reciprocated and may indeed be interpreted as naïvety unquestionably contributes to some of the resentment which is exhibited by some of the younger Hawaiians towards the out-groups in general but towards the Haoles in particular (see Chapter V). With the possible exception of the newly arrived Samoans who inherit a similar tradition of open-handedness, most of Hawaii's other ethnic groups have had longer experience within a calculating trading economy and therefore exercise greater restraint and sophistication in their relations with outsiders.

The host-guest relationship which is central to tourism obviously implies friendly consideration for the guest who presumably reciprocates by showing his appreciation for the services rendered, but it is at the same time a commercial transaction in which each participant is primarily concerned with his own welfare. The inevitable tension between these two conflicting claims may, and frequently does, lead to misunderstanding and even exploitation on either side. The tourist who is presented with a higher hotel bill than he had bargained for or whose accommodation does not measure up to his expectations is likely to conclude that the reference to the aloha spirit is a fraud—merely a form of deception to divert attention from low-level chicanery. Islanders serving the tourists, on the other hand, have learned from sad experience that special kindness to strangers is sometimes repaid by a departure with an unpaid bill or the abuse of the host's property or sensibilities and thus caution creeps into the expression of aloha. In either case, the term aloha becomes somewhat suspect.

This is not to under-rate the important part which a long tradition of friendliness and consideration towards strangers still plays in the life of the Islands. Probably because visitors

have been accustomed in their home communities to be wary
of strangers and especially of those whose outward appearance is strikingly unfamiliar, they are all the more pleasantly
surprised by the ready expressions of courtesy and kindness
which they encounter in Hawaii. Certainly this is an experience which is frequently, although by no means universally,
alluded to by visitors, and because it is approvingly com-
mented upon Islanders derive genuine satisfaction in seeking
to justify the reputation by their own conduct. Journals kept
by visiting school-teachers attending the University of Hawaii
contain references to unexpected and unsought courtesies
and expressions of concern and consideration much more
frequently than to the accounts of discourtesies and abuse,
and the same is true of the letters by tourists to the newspapers.

Such responses of kindness and regard for the stranger may
be encountered to some degree in any culture and can be
attributed to the universally human capacity of 'taking the
role of the other', under certain circumstances. It is probable
that this quality has been more extensively cultivated under
the conditions which have prevailed in Hawaii than in most
other places and that it should have been more effectively
maintained by its identification with the Hawaiian tradition
of aloha. Certainly it is not peculiar to Hawaii. That the
tourist interests, however, should have sought to capitalize
upon aloha as a quality which is unique to Hawaii is likewise
understandable.

The mounting flood of tourists becomes a threat to the
Island pattern of race relations because of the impact of
some of the associated services and the growing impersonal-
ization of life as the community grows in size. This is abun-
dantly illustrated in the experience of Waikiki, which is
still both a symbol and the major centre of tourism in Hawaii.
On an area of less than one square mile, extending from
Honolulu proper like a small island, are concentrated nearly
75 per cent of all the hotel rooms in the entire State and most
of the commercialized tourist attractions, such as night-
clubs, cabarets, bars, and restaurants. This newly created
tourist community, with its multi-storied hotels and wholly

metropolitan appearance and atmosphere, has taken shape on the horizon so suddenly as to seem to the older residents of the Islands as a foreign over-commercialized city of which they tend to disapprove. It is here that the overwhelming majority of tourists are first introduced to the Islands, where the largest and most impersonal and individualistic crowds are assembled every day and night, and where associations, including those across racial and ethnic lines, can be most casual, transitory, and also most stimulating. The tourist, immersed in this sort of an environment even for a few days, may respond with surprising facility to the psychological climate he encounters there. Thus far, the atmosphere has been predominantly conducive to a free, friendly and permissive type of communication with the resident population of all ethnic backgrounds, and it is the tourist who is more likely to be influenced than to project his outside prejudices on the Island environment, although, of course, there is some interaction in both directions. There are some observers who contend that a large influx of mainlanders as permanent residents to service the tourist population—musicians, entertainers, skilled workmen and professional personnel, especially in the large chain-hotels—will have a more disturbing effect. Again, it must be said that the dominant tendency thus far has been for these newcomers gradually, although sometimes reluctantly, to become assimilated socially and to take over for themselves the racially egalitarian practices which the Island environment seems to require. It would not be surprising, however, if some of the kindly, interpersonal atmosphere associated with the aloha spirit were also lost.

A SITUATIONAL APPROACH

The complexity of the Hawaiian racial scene, contrary to the popular impression of its idyllic simplicity, becomes most apparent once the rich and varied historical background of the Islands is even moderately penetrated. The situational nature of Hawaiian race relations is doubtless accentuated by the fact of insularity, both from continental neighbours and among the inhabitable land masses of the Hawaiian chain. Even more conducive to diversity have been the shifting phases in the economic and political life, with each of the institutional types discussed thus far dominating the relationships among the ethnic groups for its limited season and place.

No one can doubt that Hawaii's present-day reputation and experience in race relations would have been markedly different without the peculiar circumstances under which the particular elements have been brought together. As noted earlier, Hawaii's insularity at such great distances from larger island or continental neighbours has exercised a crucial part in its political destiny and consequent race relations. If Hawaii's location and resources had been such as to invite its seizure by one of the major powers early in the nineteenth century, colonialism would certainly have left its mark to a much greater degree on the subsequent relations between the invaders and the natives or the immigrant labour groups. So also, if colonialism had been further compounded by an earlier and longer history of plantation dominance, the association of the dominant racial group with the natives and immigrant groups would certainly have been far less benign and democratic. One can speculate as to the possible consequences on Island race relations of a variety of other circumstances, all of which would merely further emphasize the situational nature of Hawaii's experience.

For analytical purposes the delineation of the frontiers of race relations in Hawaii as if they were separate and independent of one another has been valid and useful, but a closer examination of the facts reveals considerable overlapping both in time and space and a consequent interaction with one another. The severity of discipline on the early plantations was considerably less in Hawaii than elsewhere because of the closer proximity of the free labour markets in the commercial centres and the existence of resident proprietors sensitive to the personal claims of their workers. Although the equalitarian atmosphere of the commerical centres has now penetrated to a greater or lesser degree into virtually every portion of the Islands, including both plantations and military installations, a reciprocal impact has also been noted. Planters of an earlier day and members of the military hierarchy more recently have frequently retired in Honolulu and have continued there to expound some of the racial attitudes expressed in their former environment. The military communities, because of their self-sufficiency and the high turnover of their personnel, have been more effectively insulated from the wider community influences but this immunity is by no means complete.

Thus, along with the strong initial and continuing impact of an equalitarian pattern of race relations, the situation in Hawaii has been strikingly fluid and flexible because of the complexity of the forces at work. The presence of such a variety of ethnic groups in Hawaii, to which many observers attribute the absence of a rigidly defined and stratified racial hierarchy, is itself a by-product of several different sets of forces, and the so-called racial groups are themselves constantly changing in complexion and status as the frontiers, which have brought them into being, interact with one another. This is the process to which our attention should now be directed.

HAWAIIAN DEFINITIONS OF RACE

The reader must have sensed long before this that the term race, as employed in the quoted references to the Hawaiian situation, does not correspond in any precise way to the dictionary or textbook definitions as 'one of the major biological divisions of mankind', or 'a population characterized by common, identifiable, and genetically transmitted physical traits'. Groupings of Island residents as loosely and variously designated as Chinese, Portuguese, Filipinos, Norwegians, Germans, Japanese, Haoles, and Hawaiians have under different circumstances and times been referred to as races.

The first racial designations were made by the native Hawaiian between himself as a Kanaka (man) and the Haole (stranger or outsider), illustrating the basic function of race as applied to man, namely as a classificatory device to distinguish between members of the in-group and the out-group. It is doubtful whether these distinctions carried any biological implications to either Kanaka or Haole, judging by the free intercourse between them and the emergence of a mixed-blood population of considerable size. The few foreigners who remained permanently in Hawaii prior to 1820—chiefly deserting sailors—tended to become Hawaiians in language, dress, and custom, and Western conceptions of race would have had little opportunity to become established in the Islands until after the settlement of a sizeable number of foreign families commencing with the arrival of the missionaries.

The early plantation strategy of recruiting diverse ethnic

groups and locating them in separate camps or communities for more effective labour control has been largely responsible, as noted in the previous chapter, for the major racial designations which have prevailed in Hawaii for close to a century. In some instances the practice of the planters to treat alike all persons recruited from the same foreign region, such as China, the Philippines, or the islands of the south and central Pacific, has served to create a sense of racial identity and solidarity where little or none existed before. Thus the labourers recruited through the port of Canton, even though they came from districts whose language and culture were quite diverse and alien to one another, such as the Hakka and Punti, were all assumed to be alike, and in the course of time they came to acquire a feeling of unity among themselves. A comparable growth in nationalistic or what is called racial unity, as a consequence of the planters having dealt with their workers as if they were culturally and linguistically alike, occurred among the more sharply differentiated Tagalogs, Visayans, and Ilocanos recruited from the Philippines.

While the plantation in Hawaii has been a peculiarly 'race-making' experience for most of the labour immigrants, according them a relatively secure status towards the bottom of the socio-economic ladder, it has been the trading frontier in particular which has provided the greatest opportunity for the immigrant and his children to escape from the racial stereotypes and to improve their socio-economic position. Throughout the greater part of the period of plantation dominance (1876–1930), as the workers completed the conditions of their contracts, the majority sought to escape either to their home land or to the expanding opportunities in and through the cities and towns. This clear succession of the major ethnic groups employed as labourers on the sugar plantations at three different intervals is reflected in Table 1. The peak in the employment of Chinese labour developed in the early 1880s, of the Japanese shortly after the turn of the century, and of the Filipinos in the early 1930s, followed a few years later by a sharp decline in the proportion of plantation workers among the first two groups. The rise and

TABLE I

PERCENTAGE DISTRIBUTION OF LABOURERS ON HAWAIIAN
SUGAR PLANTATIONS BY RACE

	1882	*1902*	*1932†*
Hawaiian and part-Hawaiian	25·1	3.5	1·2
Chinese	49.2	9·3	1·4
Japanese	·1	73·5	18·8
Portuguese	6·2	6·4	4·0
Puerto Rican	0·0	4·8	1·6
Korean	0·0	0·0	·9
Caucasian	8·1*	0·0	1·9
Filipino	0·0	0·0	69·9
All others	11·2‡	2·5	·3
Total Number	10,243	42,242	49,947

* Includes chiefly Germans and Norwegians.
† Includes men only.
‡ Consisting chiefly of South Sea Islanders.

Source: Computed from data in Romanzo Adams, *The Peoples of
Hawaii* (Honolulu, Institute of Pacific Relations, 1933), p. 36.

fall in the proportion of workers from the smaller ethnic
groups is, of course, much less dramatically reflected in
the table.

The term Haole, which had become identified with superior
economic and social status during the early days of the trading frontier when the few foreigners acquired positions of
special power and prestige by virtue of their technological
skills and knowledge, is noticeably lacking from the racial
types listed among plantation labourers. The Haoles on the
plantations were the small group in proprietary and mana-
gerial positions whose influence appeared to depend in
some instances on their ability to keep the workers at a
distance through the barriers of race. Hence even groups
which in the strict biological interpretation of race were akin
to the promoting group, such as the Germans, Norwegians,
Poles, Russians and Spanish, who came to Hawaii as
labourers, were designated as separate racial groups while
on the plantations, and it was not until they moved into the
less class-conscious atmosphere of the city, or the plantation

had developed to its later stages, that they were able to become associated with the Haole community. The more numerous Portuguese have undergone a somewhat similar experience, continuing to be designated as a separate group with a relatively unchanged status on the plantations but merging with the Haole community in the urban centres. Persons of Spanish and Portuguese ancestry were classified in separate 'racial' categories, as distinct from Other Caucasians (Haoles) in the U.S. census enumerations of 1910, 1920 and 1930 in conformity with Island practice, especially on the plantations, but by 1940 the situation had changed sufficiently through intermarriage and an exodus to the cities apparently to justify the combination of all three groups under the general term of Caucasians.

The combined influence of the trading frontier, the plantation and the political controls emanating from continental United States are apparent in the racial categories utilized in Table 2. At the time of the first official 'Complete Census' in 1853 and again in 1860 and 1866, the native terms to differentiate between Islanders and outsiders (Kanaka and Haole) were still employed, but in the English translation, deemed necessary for the growing cosmopolitan community, the indigenes were designated as Native, Part-Native, or Half-Caste. The term half-caste, used in each Census from 1866 to 1890, and the Hawaiian equivalent used earlier of *Hapa-haole* or half-foreign, both carry a mild note of discrimination which is hardly consistent with the equalitarian emphasis of the trading frontier. The categories under which foreigners were further classified had from the beginning a regional or national rather than a biological connotation, and this tendency was further re-enforced later by the encouragement of such distinctions on the plantations. The appearance in the table of most of the national categories corresponds with the introduction of workers from these areas.

Racial categories, however, in the conventional Western sense of large groupings of people sharing common recognizable and genetically inherited physical traits did not appear in the Hawaiian census until the Islands were

TABLE 2

POPULATION IN HAWAII BY RACE, 1853–1960

	1853		1884		1910		1930		1950		1960	
	No.	%	No.	%	No.	%	No.	%	No.	%	No.	%
Hawaiian (Kanaka – native)	70,036	95.8	40,014	49.7	26,041	13.6	22,636	6.1	12,245	2.5	10,502	1.7
Part-Hawaiian (Hapa haole–half-caste)	983	1.3	4,218	5.2	12,506	6.5	28,224	7.7	73,845	14.8	91,597	14.5
Caucasian	87	.1	9,967	12.3	39,158	20.4	73,702	20.0	114,793	23.0	202,230	32.0
Portuguese					22,301	11.6	27,588	7.5				
Other Caucasian (Haole)	1,600*	2.2	6,612*	8.3	14,867	7.7	44,895	12.2				
Chinese	364	.5	18,254	22.6	21,674	11.3	27,179	7.4	32,376	6.5	38,119	6.0
Japanese			116	.1	79,675	41.5	139,631	37.9	184,598	36.9	203,876	32.2
Korean					4,533	2.4	6,461	1.8	7,030	1.4		
Filipino					2,361	1.2	63,052	17.1	61,062	12.2	68,641	10.8
Puerto Rican					4,890	2.5	6,671	1.8	9,551	1.9		
Negro	5				695	.4	563	.2	2,651	.5	4,943	.8
All other	62	.1	1,397	1.7	376	.2	217	.1	1,618	.3	12,864	2.0
Total	73,137		80,578		191,909		368,336		499,769		632,772	

* Consists chiefly of persons born in the United States and the countries of north-western Europe, and their children born in Hawaii.

Source: Adapted from data in Andrew W. Lind, *Hawaii's People* (Honolulu, University of Hawaii Press, 1967), p. 28.

annexed by the United States. For example, in the 1853
Census the presence of twenty Negroes among the foreign
residents was mentioned in a footnote, but they were not
separately classified in the same way as persons from
France, the United States, or other regions of the world.
Later, when the number of children born in Hawaii of
foreign parentage became large enough to require special
attention, persons of Chinese, French, Micronesian, or
American ancestry, without regard to their biological
heritage, were all included within a common classification.
Immediately following annexation, however, Mainland
racial definitions were imposed on the Hawaiian Census
terminology and the terms Caucasian and Negro were for
the first time introduced. This had the effect in the 1900
Census of throwing together under the hodge-podge category of Caucasian three locally significant groupings of
Haoles, Portuguese, and light-complexioned part-Hawaiians.
Although the biologically tinged terms continued to be
employed in the subsequent censuses and even in the tabula-
tion of vital statistics within the Islands, provision was made
in the population enumerations of 1910, 1920, and 1930 to
take account of local conceptions of race. It became the
practice then to differentiate among the plantation-
imported Portuguese and Spanish, the part-Hawaiians, and
the persons of European or American ancestry enjoying
Haole status, the latter being classified under the anomalous
designation of Other Caucasian.

The most serious violation of Island traditions with respect
to race occurred in 1960 when U.S. mainland designations
were applied in their entirety to Hawaii, as they were to the
other forty-nine states of the Union. Thus, the conception
incorporated in the U.S. Census of Population which identi-
fies race with colour and provides a major distinction only
between white and non-white was not only completely alien
to Hawaii but established a dichotomy which was virtually
meaningless in the Island setting. To combine into a single
category such groupings as the Chinese, Japanese, Korean,
Filipinos, Hawaiians, and part-Hawaiians as distinguished
from the Caucasians is clearly to do violence to some of the

most significant aspects of contemporary life in Hawaii. The
very limited data in the 1960 Census organized on the basis
of race rather than colour take account only of the three
categories which were thought to be most significant on the
American continent—White, Negro, and Other Races—
but very little is gained by a threefold classification, since
the Negro portion of Hawaii's population is so extremely
small.

The greater part of the statistical substance in Table 2
is less directly relevant at this juncture than the categories
which have been used in the classification of the data. The
shifting numerical size, however, has been an important
factor in whether or not a group is recognized as a separate
racial entity. For example, had it not been for the requirement imposed by the U.S. Census Bureau that a separate
category for the Negro be included in the enumeration
schedule, it is doubtful whether the Islanders' awareness of
this racial group would have justified the inclusion of this
category until the census of 1950, if then. Certainly the
small number which had come to Hawaii except under the
emergency conditions of the two world wars and the Korean
and Vietnam crises have given Islanders little consciousness
of Negroes as a distinct racial group in their midst. This is
especially true on the islands other than Oahu where the
few permanent Negro residents are almost wholly concentrated.

The adoption by Islanders of the term Caucasian as a
substitute for, or an addition to, the term Haole has occurred
somewhat more readily owing to the sizeable immigration
since 1930 of military and civilian personnel whose economic
status is below that formerly attributed to the Haole. Ethnic
groups such as the Portuguese, Koreans, Puerto Ricans and
the recently arrived Samoans, which have been either
dropped from, or never included in, the census listing, still
stand out clearly in popular consciousness as distinct and
separate entities. The very rapid expansion in numbers and
in the proportion of the total population among the
Japanese—from 0·1 per cent of the total in 1884 to 41·5
per cent in 1910—has, of course, figured prominently in

the public concern as to their presence. So also, the decline
in the proportion of the pure Hawaiians from 95·8 per cent
of the total population in 1853 to 1·7 per cent in 1960 has
paradoxically focused increased attention on them as victims
of Western civilization and exploitation. The corresponding
growth in the mixed-blood offspring of the Hawaiians,
which is even more striking numerically than the decline of
pure Hawaiians, is much less commonly recognized.

The conceptions of race incorporated in the official
censuses are, of course, not the only ones; neither are they
necessarily those which are most widely prevalent or most
commonly adhered to in the community. The fact of official
practice and acceptance does, nevertheless, give them a
sanction and influence which cannot be denied. Even the
application to Hawaii of the U.S. census policy of differenti-
ating only between white and non-white and of virtually
disregarding the Island distinctions among the various
ethnic groups seems to give support to the sentiment that
racial distinctions ought to be abandoned entirely as being
inconsistent with American professions of democracy. A
number of official agencies in the Islands, such as the public
schools, the Department of Social Services, and some of the
courts, have adopted a policy of disregarding race in any
public reports, although effective functioning has commonly
required keeping a record of the racial ancestry of their
clients. On the other hand, some public and private agencies
have found it expedient not only to take account of race in
their confidential relations with members of the community,
but also in their reporting of their activities to the general
public.

What seems to emerge most strikingly from this analysis
is that the so-called races of Hawaii are in reality groupings
of people sharing common cultural and physical traits by
which they can be recognized. All of Hawaii's racial groups,
with the exception of the Hawaiians and their mixed-blood
descendants, were originally in some sense invaders of the
Islands, whether they came on their own initiative or were
recruited by others. The newcomers acquire a racial
character in the Hawaiian sense whenever their physical

appearance and conduct are so distinctive as to be interpreted by themselves and others as genetically acquired—as rooted in the germ plasm. Thus races come into being and races cease to exist, not because a new breed is born or an old stock dies out, but because the shifting conditions of life have made such groups clearly conscious of their being significantly different from others and have enforced a comparable conviction upon those who do not belong. The races of Hawaii, like those in most other parts of the world, have had to be discovered or even invented; they do not necessarily have substance in and of themselves, and they tend to disappear when they or others no longer take account of them.

CHANGING SOCIAL STATUS

The one all-consuming purpose in coming to Hawaii for the great majority of the immigrants was to capture as much as possible of the wealth of the Islands and then return to the home land to enjoy the prestige and material comforts which the wealth could buy for themselves and their kin folk. But in this respect, they were not notably different from the people brought together in many, if not most, of the areas of race and culture contacts of the modern world. If Hawaii differs from other areas in this phase of the experience, it is chiefly in the manner and the extent to which this goal has been gratified. The struggle within and across racial barriers for economic survival and advancement is in any case a central consideration in the analysis of Island race relations, involving both natives as well as immigrants.

For the great bulk of the immigrants to Hawaii the initial phase of this struggle was one involving chiefly their own survival, with racial considerations figuring only slightly. The demand for cheap, unskilled workers, in response to which most of the immigrants came to Hawaii, exceeded the available supply throughout the greater part of the plantation era, and able-bodied persons of all ethnic groups could always find employment, if they were willing to accept the conditions of labour, including the relatively meagre income and the frequently inadequate living conditions. Racially segregated camps and work gangs during the early plantation period reduced the likelihood of inter-racial confrontations, except with the Haole directing group whose power and influence the workers were in no position to contest.

Substantial differences did occur, however, in the wages and living conditions received by workers of different ethnic groups, but this cannot be attributed exclusively to racial discrimination. Bargaining conditions existing in the home land at the time the contracts were drawn up, as well as ascertained inadequacies in worker efficiency, may have figured prominently in differences which appear in Table 3.

TABLE 3

COST OF PLANTATION FIELD LABOUR IN HAWAII, 1886 AND 1890

Nationality of workers	Cost to planters, 1886		Wages per month for men, without food	
	Board per month	Quarters	1886	1890
Chinese	$6.43	$31.49	$13.56	$17.54
Japanese	6.32	41.94	9.88	17.21
South Sea Islanders	5.77	46.10	10.16	17.19
Portuguese	9.16	76.38	10.41	20.89
Germans	8.00	79.57	12.75	26.02
Norwegians	10.00	31.00	9.00	26.02

Source: Report of the Commissioner of Labor on Hawaii (Washington, Government Printing Office, 1902), p. 81.

Towards the end of the plantation era, discrepancies in the wages paid to the different ethnic groups still persisted in both the salaried (preferred) and non-salaried categories, although these differences were much more evident in the preferred occupations. All the earnings recorded in Table 4 seem pitifully low in terms of present-day standards, but the fact still remains, as Francis Maxwell reported just a few years earlier, that 'among the cane countries employing

TABLE 4

AVERAGE MONTHLY AND ANNUAL EARNINGS AMONG SALARIED
AND NON-SALARIED WORKERS BY RACE, 1938†

Race‡	Monthly earnings		Annual earnings	
	Non-salaried workers	Salaried workers	Non-salaried workers	Salaried workers
Filipino	$46.92	$67.08	$489	$802
Japanese	50.94	76.94	628	924
Portuguese	56.23	86.75	629	1,038
Hawaiian and Part-Hawaiian	54.07	—*	573	—*
Puerto Rican	44.96	64.94	536	—*
Haole	76.00	137.91	786	1,558
Chinese	42.39	90.56	487	—*
Total	48.88	85.06	546	1,011

* Number too few to compute averages.

† Data derived from *Labor in the Territory of Hawaii, 1939*. Perquisites, including fuel, light, water, and medical services, are not included.

‡ Arranged in order of the number of persons employed.

Source: Data derived from *Labor in the Territory of Hawaii, 1939* (Washington, United States Department of Labor, Bureau of Labor Statistics, 1939), pp. 52, 53, 63.

coloured labour, the Hawaiian Islands pay, on the whole, the highest wages, and moreover, spend most in attending to the welfare of the labourers'.[1] Such factors as the relatively recent arrival in the Islands of the Filipinos and their greater transiency as workers, and the advanced age of the few Chinese still employed as labourers explain in part the disparities among the groups from the Orient. The strikingly higher earnings of Haoles among both salaried and non-salaried workers strongly suggest that racial considerations were at least partially responsible. This was probably also a factor in the advantage enjoyed by the Portuguese and to a lesser degree by the Hawaiians, most of whom were of mixed ancestry.

[1] Francis Maxwell, *Economic Aspects of Cane Sugar Production* (London, 1927), p. 88.

E

Whatever bases there may once have been for discrimination in the wages paid to workers of different ethnic groups
on Hawaii's plantations are almost wholly removed under
the changed conditions since World War II. Unquestionably
the most important factor contributing to the virtual elimination of racial considerations in wage rates and employment on the plantations was the rapid unionization of
workers in the industry in the late 1940s, immediately
following the war. The awakening of labour leaders to the
strategy which employers had utilized so successfully
throughout the plantation era, of pitting one racial group
against another as a means of combating demands of workers
for higher wages or improved living conditions—the familiar
device of 'divide and conquer'—led to the inevitable counter-
strategy of organizing workers without regard to racial background and of insisting upon racial equality within the
union.[2] The survival of strong in-group loyalties, born in
part from the racial segregation which had been so long
encouraged in plantation living, obviously delayed the
realization of this ideal in practice. Several plantation strikes,
in 1946, 1947, and 1958, uniting the workers of all ethnic
backgrounds in a common struggle against their employers,
did much to reduce if not to eliminate the racial barriers
within the unions.

The far wider range of occupational opportunities and
the greater freedom of movement outside the plantation led
also to the possibility of racial tensions on these less disci-
plined frontiers. If the immigrants had been content to
remain indefinitely in the role of docile plantation workers
there probably would have been little criticism of them on
economic grounds, but the fact that such a large proportion
of them, especially those of Oriental ancestry, began moving
into competitive occupations outside led eventually to
resentments towards the invaders.

Mild criticism from official quarters developed towards
the initial group of Chinese, who had been imported in 1852,
for their unwillingness 'to stick to their lasts' and their dis-

[2] David E. Thompson, 'The ILWU as a Force for Interracial Unity in
Hawaii', *Social Process in Hawaii* (no. 15, 1951), pp. 32–43.

position whenever possible 'to live without work—by store-keeping, perhaps'. Actually storekeeping was the occupation most readily accessible to the newcomers as the first step on their own initiative towards higher economic and social status in the new country, and immigrant groups around the world, as well as in Hawaii, to whom other occupational outlets might be denied, have found this one field in which they could secure a foothold. No major resentment towards the Chinese developed at that time, owing to their limited numbers and the fact that the needed services they undertook as pedlars and small tradesmen were not otherwise being provided.

Within another thirty years, however, 29 per cent of the Chinese population in the Islands had established residence in the city of Honolulu and their economic adjustment there could only be described by a missionary observer as follows:

The Chinese have the very qualities which the Hawaiians most lack—industry, providence, . . . subtlety—all the money-saving virtues are with the Chinese. Idleness, carelessness, generosity, simplicity, all the money-losing qualities are with the Hawaiians. . . . Nothing is more absolutely sure than this: that as a laborer, small farmer, shop-keeper, and tradesman, the Chinaman will crowd the native Hawaiian to the wall, and will take his place, but he is doing this peaceably, and with the Hawaiian's tacit consent. . . . There is much more probability of an open conflict between the Chinese and the Anglo-Saxon (Haole). Anglo-Saxon mechanics and tradesmen are, every month, being brought more and more into competition with Chinamen. If you will ride slowly through the Chinese quarter . . . you will find watch-maker's and jeweller's shops, tinshops, shoe-shops, tailorshops, saddle and harness-shops, furniture shops, cabinet shops, and bakeries, all run by Chinamen with Chinese workmen. While in the Chinese stores, which crowd each other in the Chinese quarter, and dot every street throughout the city and country you can find anything you want, from a stove or a shawl, down through drugs, groceries, notions, and what-not, to the little 3 feet by 7 den, where you could carry the entire stock on your back and not be very heavily laden either.[3]

[3] 'The Chinese in Hawaii', *The Friend* (Vol. 31, no. 11, 1882), pp. 115-16.

As early as 1869 the competition of Chinese tradesmen and skilled workers in Honolulu had evoked bitter opposition from Haoles and natives 'who saw their field invaded and their profits threatened by the cheap labor of the Chinese',[4] but nothing more serious than a series of mass meetings to protest further importations from China developed at that time.

By the middle 1880s when 61 per cent of the operators of retail establishments in the Islands were Chinese, vigorous adverse sentiments towards them had broken into the open especially among the white population of the Islands, and legislation was enacted in 1886 prohibiting further labour importation of Chinese after 1888. The motivating bases for further legislative restrictions on the Chinese during the last two decades of the century are objectively stated in the missionary journal as follows:

Many thousands of Chinese laborers have been imported into these islands under contract to work on the sugar plantations. On the expiration of their terms of contract, a majority of these laborers seek other employment. Many of them become mechanics and tradesmen. They are able to live on a fraction of what is necessary for white men in the same employments, and are extremely patient and assiduous in toil. Hence they are generally able to crowd out white mechanics and clerks, especially in the lower grades of these occupations.

From the white man's point of view, this is necessarily regarded as a great evil. The white mechanic will not fail to see it a great grievance that his employment is taken from him, and his rate of wages forced down by Chinese labor. This grievance is a genuine one and cannot be ignored on any plea of philanthropic regard for men of other races, as is apt to be done without proper discrimination by writers residing on the Atlantic Coast.[5]

As additional preferred occupational outlets developed for the Chinese, and competitors from other ethnic groups emerged from the plantations, the heat of adverse sentiment towards the Chinese declined greatly and never again reached the intensity of the late nineteenth century.

Other ethnic groups have undergone much the same type of experience as they have emerged from the level of planta-

---

[4] *Report of the President of the Board of Education*, Honolulu, 1886, p. 35.
[5] 'Chinese Restriction', *The Friend* (Vol. 52, no. 3, 1894), p. 24.

tion labourers. The first step into one or another of a variety
of relatively menial and poorly remunerated occupations,
such as domestic service, huckstering and unskilled labour,
usually encountered little opposition or resentment since
the immigrant still remained pretty much 'in his place'. On
the other hand, it did provide the immigrant with a degree
of freedom and independence not available on the plantations and was valued as such. The movement into better
paying and more highly respected occupations was almost
certain to elicit opposition, particularly if any large numbers were involved, as in the case of the Japanese. Thus, the
sheer increase in the number of Japanese from 116 or 0·1 per
cent of the total population of Hawaii in 1884 to 24,407 or
22·4 per cent of the total just twelve years later and to 61,111
or 39·6 per cent in 1900 did draw forth some dire predictions
as to the consequences of such a radical transformation in
the racial complexion of the Islands, but the substantial
shift of Japanese into domestic service and unskilled jobs
outside the plantations during the same period did not
occasion any great amount of adverse sentiment. During the
following decade, however, as Japanese moved into the skilled
trades and merchandizing the criticism became intense.

A considerable portion of the 1905 report on labour conditions in Hawaii by the U.S. Department of Labor was
devoted to an exposition of the 'Orientalization of laboring
population and its results', although primarily attention was
directed to the invasion by the Japanese in trade and the
skilled occupations:

... the Orientalization of the islands is reacting more disastrously
on the white and native wage-earners, merchants, and even
farmers, than it is on the planters. . . . The first effect of the
incoming of the Asiatics was the taking over of unskilled labor of
every sort, but the competition has now extended until it has
become active in nearly every line of trade and in nearly all the
skilled occupations. Most of the competition in the skilled trades
comes from the Japanese, and it is insisted everywhere throughout the islands that this competition is growing rapidly.[6]

⁶ 'Third Report of the Commissioner of Labor on Hawaii', *Bulletin of the
Bureau of Labor* (Washington, U.S. Printing Office, September 1906), p. 383.

The report continues in a similar vein, stressing especially the acute struggle in the building and technical trades, 'where white contractors had been ruinously underbid by Japanese contractors or by white contractors using Asiatic labor exclusively'.

Many large employers are decidedly opposed to having a Japanese on their force for the very reason that they realize that they are training up future competitors in their business. 'I won't teach men to cut my throat,' was a typical expression from a large employer. . . . It is not easy to give an adequate idea of the resentment and the bitterness felt by the white mechanic and the white merchant who see themselves forced to the wall, and even driven out of the Territory, by Asiatic competition. They feel they are being defeated in the struggle . . . because of a lower plane of living, in the face of which they are helpless. They feel, furthermore, that the white citizen who goes into new American territory to cast his lot with a new community is entitled, if not to a favored treatment, at least, to protection against the kind of competition that the Asiatic alien represents.[7]

The gentleman's agreement in 1907 between the United States and Japan had an immediate alleviating effect on the tensions in Hawaii by eliminating further large-scale labour immigration from Japan. On the other hand, the large number of Japanese in Hawaii, exceeding that of any other ethnic group throughout the first six decades of the present century, together with the fact that many of their basic moral values, such as industry and initiative, so closely paralleled those of their American and European rivals, made the Japanese seem to be a constant threat to those holding the preferred positions in the Islands. Any combined activities among the Japanese, such as mutual-aid societies (*kumi*), language schools, and Buddhist temples or Shinto shrines, might be interpreted as menacing to the established order, and such major organized efforts as the plantation strikes of 1909 and 1920 or the 'language-school litigation' of the middle 1920s seemed clearly to confirm latent fears of a racial conspiracy and caused the temporary breaking of the

[7] 'Third Report of the Commissioner of Labor on Hawaii', op. cit., pp. 388, 392.

Island taboo on the public criticism of any group on the basis of its racial origin. Such major crises have been relatively few in number and during the intervals between them the traditional controls have prevailed.

The upward mobility of Japanese during the post-plantation period—from about 1930 onwards—has involved chiefly persons of Island birth and heritage, and whatever threat their larger numbers might offer to the established order could not be attacked on the basis of their being of foreign birth. The Japanese, as well as the other immigrant groups from the Orient, have placed a high value on learning and have, therefore, availed themselves of the free or low-cost public education afforded in Hawaii to a greater degree than the immigrants from other parts of the world or than the natives. The second and third generation children of the Japanese have to a considerable degree acquired the qualifications to assume positions further up the economic scale than their immigrant parents. Vigorous opposition was expressed by members of the Haole élite, particularly the planters, to the mounting costs of free public education for the increasing numbers of immigrant children because, so it was claimed, they were thereby being enticed away from the humble stations in life to which they had been born and expectations were encouraged which the existing social order did not seem to justify.

Some indication of the potential conflict inherent in this later phase of the upward movement among persons of Oriental ancestry in Hawaii was provided in a prophetic statement by Romanzo Adams in the late 1920s as follows:

The Occidental men have been sitting in the seats of power. They have developed those abilities and those attitudes that normally result from conscious exercise of power. The Orientals in Hawaii . . . have had to accept a position of inferior privilege and power. . . . They have worked to the plans of others or have engaged in the minor economic activities. . . . They have done a large share of the hard work while enjoying relatively little of the comforts and luxuries. . . . In Hawaii, as in the larger area [of the Pacific], the Oriental has accepted his position as a temporary expedient. If the Occidental flattered himself into believing that his superior status was the result of superior native capacity, the Oriental did not agree with him. Now the Orientals in Hawaii and elsewhere are acquiring scientific knowledge. . . . They are demanding with ever increasing articulateness that there be a readjustment of social relationships on such a basis that a man of any race may have opportunity according to his ability without adverse racial discrimination . . . this demand for a recognition or assumption of race equality generates conflict.[8]

Adams' reference to Orientals related primarily to the Japanese, whose young people constituted nearly 45 per cent of those aged 10 to 19 years in Hawaii in 1930, but his characterization specifically of the Japanese boys applied with equal validity to those of Chinese, Korean, or Filipino ancestry who had preceded, were contemporaries of, or were to follow the Japanese by a few years:

Thousands of boys born on the plantations are rather suddenly appearing on the scene as active competitors for the preferred jobs. Moreover, their ability, industry, and character is such that many of them are pretty sure to win an improved status if they are given an even chance or even if they are placed under conditions of moderately adverse discrimination. This accentuates competition all along the line.[9]

There is, indeed, considerable evidence that the 'moderately adverse' circumstances under which most of Hawaii's Orientals of that period had to compete did, in fact, act as a spur to greater effort and achievement than if they had been lacking, whereas the young Haoles and some of the youth in other ethnic groups, from their favoured position of better educational and economic opportunities, were denied the stimulation of adversity. There was in the case of Oriental youth the added motivation of family pride and loyalty by which the second generation, with the advantages of a Western education, sought to realize the economic and social dreams which had brought their parents to Hawaii but which so many had failed to achieve.

[8] Romanzo Adams, *The Education of the Boys of Hawaii and Their Economic Outlook*, University of Hawaii Research Publications, no. 4 (January 1928), pp. 6–7.

[9] Ibid., p. 18.

The census of occupations over the past half century reveals somewhat more objectively the manner and the extent to which Hawaii's racial groups have succeeded in taking advantage of the expanding economic opportunities in the Islands. Despite the lack of consistency in the categories utilized over the fifty-year period, a clear trend towards greater equality across ethnic lines appears in the data of Table 5. Using only the two contrasting categories of labour and professions towards the bottom and the top of the occupational hierarchy, there is evident a clear trend among the

TABLE 5

PERCENTAGE OF EMPLOYED MALES BY ETHNIC GROUP AND
MAJOR OCCUPATIONS, 1910, 1930, 1950, AND 1960

Ethnic group	Occupation	Census period			
		1910	*1930*	*1950*	*1960*
All groups	Labour	65·0	53·6	22·5	15·6
	Professions	1·1	3·4	7·3	10·2
Hawaiians	Labour	50·5	39·5	34·6	*
	Professions	1·6	4·1	3·6	*
Part-Hawaiians	Labour	24·9	22·1	20·0	*
	Professions	3·1	6·7	6·3	*
Portuguese	Labour	*	30·1	*	*
	Professions	*	2·6	*	*
Caucasian	Labour	43·8	4·4†	5·1	8·4
	Professions	3·1	17·2†	16·9	17·9
Chinese	Labour	48·6	24·4	5·3	4·4
	Professions	·5	3·0	10·7	16·6
Japanese	Labour	76·8	35·9	16·3	9·9
	Professions	·5	3·4	5·5	10·1
Filipino	Labour	*	90·1	52·5	40·0
	Professions	*	·6	1·2	1·8
Korean	Labour	*	53·4	11·4	*
	Professions	*	2·7	8·6	*
Puerto Rican	Labour	*	78·2	34·4	*
	Professions	*	1·1	·9	*

* Not separately listed.
† Haole only.

Source: Data derived from Lind, *Hawaii's People*, pp. 77, 80.

entire population of Hawaii away from the less desired towards the more desired fields, paralleling, of course, the
trend throughout the Western world.

Virtually all of the immigrant ethnic groups have undergone a decline in the proportion of their employed male
population engaged as ordinary labourers, the earlier
arriving Chinese having moved farther than any of the
others and the latest arriving Filipinos continued to provide from 1930 onwards a wholly disproportionate number
in what is usually regarded as the least desired category.

The mounting proportions of the immigrant groups in the
professions are drawn overwhelmingly from among the
Island-born and Western-educated generations, with the
Chinese greatly exceeding the average and all other groups
except the Caucasians. Although the Filipinos had some
representation in the professions throughout the period of
their residence in Hawaii, it has always been slight and as
recently as 1960 was less than one-fifth of what it would be
if the Filipinos were represented in proportion to their
number in the total population. Of the two immigrant
groups which had arrived in Hawaii at about the same time,
towards the beginning of the present century, the Koreans
had moved out of the labour category and into the preferred
professional class to a far greater degree than the Puerto
Ricans, who lagged very much behind the average in both
areas. Neither the Hawaiians nor the part-Hawaiians have
experienced the rising trend in occupational status comparable to that observed among the Oriental immigrant groups.
In fact, the pure Hawaiians had dropped from a slightly
preferred position as compared with the total in 1910 to
one below the average in 1950 (see Chapter IV).

Still another objective index of the trend towards the
equalization in economic position across ethnic lines is
found in the Census returns on income as recorded in Table
6. Most of the immigrants had come to Hawaii with the
hope of winning a fortune or at least of earning a better
livelihood than was possible in the native community, and
consequently they and their relatives at home have been
disposed to measure their success in Hawaii largely in terms

of their monetary accumulations. Although data on the distribution of incomes for specific years give little indication of the accumulated wealth, the statistics in Table 6 re-enforce the impressions derived from a variety of other sources. The rapid mounting in affluence of the entire community in the post-war period is only faintly reflected in the increase of the median income from $2,340 in 1949 to $3,717 in 1959 and only moderately well in the rise in the proportion of males receiving incomes of $5,000 or more, from 9·2 per cent in 1949 to 33·2 per cent in 1959.

In the light of the impression which still prevails in some circles in Hawaii, and the undoubted fact of an earlier period, that Haoles are invariably persons of wealth, it is worth noting that the median income of the Caucasian group which includes the Haoles was only moderately above the average in 1949 and actually below the average in 1959. On the other hand, the proportion of Caucasian males in the highest income bracket was twice as high as the average in 1949 and somewhat over one and a half times the average in 1959.

These statistics also reveal that the Chinese, who a century earlier were almost wholly confined to the bottom rungs of the economic ladder, had obtained the highest median incomes among the major ethnic groups in both 1949 and 1959. The stories of a score of second generation Chinese, the sons of immigrant labourers, who have made rapid progress since the war into the millionaire class and to membership and even the presidencies of leading economic and social agencies have already become legends in the community. There have been somewhat less dramatic instances among the second generation of Japanese ancestry, perhaps because the disposition to gamble on high stakes appears to be less developed among them. Nevertheless, by 1959, the median income of the Japanese, as well as of the Chinese, was significantly above that of the Caucasians.

The retention of traditional values, in which the accumulation of monetary wealth and the traits of character essential to it do not enjoy any special prestige, explains in large part the relatively low income among the Hawaiians and part-Hawaiians, significantly lower among the former than among the latter. The Puerto Ricans also have fared rather poorly in the economic struggle, owing in part to a cultural heritage which has not placed a great deal of emphasis upon success in a competitive urban economy. The low income level among the Filipinos is a function of their being the last of the major immigrant groups to arrive in Hawaii and their high disproportion of males and consequent lack of stable family life.

A sample survey conducted by the Hawaii Department of Health of family incomes on the island of Oahu in 1964–6 confirms in general and also amplifies the account already given. The annual median incomes of families by the ethnic stock of the head were reported for the larger groups as follows:

Chinese	$9,372	Haole (Other Caucasian)	$7,246
Japanese	$8,877	Portuguese	$6,250
Filipino	$6,087	Part-Hawaiian	$6,850
		Hawaiian	$5,583

When the data for the Haole group are further differentiated between the civilian and military families, the returns for the former become $10,319 and for the latter, $5,278—a figure even lower than that of the pure Hawaiians. These data also reflect the persistence of the economic class distinction between Portuguese and the Haoles and the even more pronounced difference within the Haole group itself.

There have been no rigid or prescribed channels through which the upward movement of the various racial groups has necessarily proceeded. For the Oriental groups, as indicated earlier, trade has provided one effective avenue. The Filipinos, however, have found this field already well occupied and have instead relied on the service and semi-skilled occupations as stepping-stones to higher status. For the Hawaiians and part-Hawaiians, mechanical occupations have apparently offered a special attraction. Such factors as the order of arrival, the length of residence in Hawaii, and the cultural tastes and traditions, especially with reference to education, of the various groups have influenced to a

TABLE 6

PERCENTAGE OF MALES RECEIVING INCOMES IN 1949, 1959 BY RACE AND INCOME CLASSES

	Up to $999	$1,000–1,999	$2,000–2,999	$3,000–3,999	$4,000–4,999	$5,000–6,999	$7,000–9,999	$10,000 and over	Median income
All races									
1949	16·6	22·3	27·1	17·6	6·9	5·3	2·1	1·8	$2,340
1959	11·3	14·4	12·2	16·0	13·0	18·0	8·7	6·5	3,717
Caucasian									
1949	9·7	24·8	17·8	18·3	10·1	11·0	4·6	3·7	2,856
1959	7·9	21·5	11·9	12·7	10·9	14·5	9·9	10·6	3,649
Chinese									
1949	17·6	14·9	20·2	22·9	11·9	7·5	3·4	3·5	2,964
1959	10·8	7·0	6·9	10·2	13·7	26·1	15·4	9·8	5,096
Japanese									
1949	17·5	17·3	29·6	21·1	6·8	3·7	1·4	1·5	2,427
1959	12·5	8·4	8·9	15·4	15·8	24·2	9·7	5·0	4,302
Filipino									
1949	18·1	32·6	40·2	7·6	1·2	·5	·1	·1	1,995
1959	14·5	11·6	22·0	28·0	11·7	9·5	2·3	·5	3,071
Hawaiian*									
1949	26·8	20·4	28·2	17·2	5·1	1·7	·4	·3	2,097
Part-Hawaiian*									
1949	21·5	16·5	25·0	22·6	7·7	4·2	1·8	·8	2,455
Puerto Rican*									
1949	23·6	21·4	34·2	16·4	2·9	1·3	·2	—	2,131

* Data available only for 1949.

Source: Lind, *Hawaii's People*, p. 100.

marked degree the rate and direction of their rise in economic position and social status. All groups, however, have participated to a greater or lesser degree and at differing times in the movement towards a higher plane of living in accordance with their own cultural tastes. Differences in the economic rewards received by the various ethnic groups obviously still exist, but, with the one notable exception of the native Polynesians, to be discussed in the next chapter, these are far less pronounced than the class differences within each of these groups, and by virtue of living so largely within a common social environment the economic distinctions across race lines tend to diminish with each passing decade.

IV | Folk People in an Industrialized World

Among the many hypotheses advanced to interpret Hawaii's race relations, the ones most readily appealing to laymen focus understandably upon the nature of the people who have been brought together there. Even when a theory of climatic influences, operating over centuries through the processes of natural selection and survival, is drawn upon as a supplementary interpretation, the notion that groups of people called races behave the way they do because they were 'born that way' seems natural and logical. The Polynesian natives especially, residents of Hawaii for at least 900 years, seem to provide the ordinary observer with the perfect example of the way in which a gentle and benign environment over the centuries has worked its selective influence on the race of hardy seafarers—'Vikings of the Sunrise', to use Sir Peter Buck's[1] colourful, if not too precise, term—who first settled these islands. 'Nature and Nurture' are commonly recognized as being interrelated in Hawaiian character, with 'sunshine and ease of sustenance' having softened and ultimately bred out any warlike disposition and incorporating instead within the basic temperament the sunshine of the aloha spirit.

Because the Hawaiians have been so commonly credited with literally 'breeding' the friendliness for which the Islands and its people generally are also widely acclaimed, some further attention may properly be directed to this particular theory. In the earlier discussion of the Hawaiians and the aloha spirit, the primary concern was the tourist

[1] Sir Peter Buck, *Vikings of the Sunrise* (London, Whitcombe and Tombs Ltd., 1938).

industry and the way in which its role was affected thereby. Our focus of attention in this chapter will be instead on the Hawaiians themselves and more particularly upon their role in the race relations of the Islands. Moreover the experience of the Hawaiians parallels in so many respects that of natives in other island areas throughout the Pacific, although in Hawaii the natives have constituted the major exception to the pattern of life to which most of the immigrant groups became early committed and which is now assumed to be dominant in the Islands.

WHAT IS UNIQUE ABOUT HAWAIIANS?

Prior to the coming of the Caucasians to these islands in 1778, the Hawaiians constituted one of the fairly numerous people of that period to whom some social scientists have applied the term 'folk' in contrast to the far wider range of peasant and metropolitan peoples.[2] By virtue of their extreme isolation over such an extended period of time, the residents of Hawaii, like those of other island areas in the Pacific, had developed a culture peculiar to themselves and the conditions of their habitat. Life in such communities was highly localized and stabilized through custom, since the means of livelihood were the resources of land and sea immediately at hand—those of a subsistence economy. In such communities, according to Redfield:

> The incentives to work and to exchange labor and goods are . . . various and chiefly noneconomic (in the narrow sense). They arise from tradition, from a sense of obligation coming out of one's position in a system of status relationships, especially those of kinship, and from religious considerations and moral motivations of many kinds.[3]

Inherent in communities so structured is an intricate web of obligations and expectations binding all people together in a homogeneous and self-sufficient whole, in which mutual

[2] This threefold system of classifying peoples and communities around the world is especially associated with the name of Robert Redfield in whose writings this scheme has been greatly elaborated.

[3] Robert Redfield, *The Primitive World and Its Transformations* (Cornell University Press, 1953), p. 11.

hospitality and generosity are central and guiding principles, so deeply rooted in the mores that no one would question them nor would they need to be taught. The ready sharing of one's substance in a subsistence economy was not only natural but essential for the survival of the group, and even the stranger, in contrast to the enemy, was shown generosity on the grounds that one might be entertaining divinity unawares.

So completely taken for granted was this mutuality in living—of sharing one's abundance with any who lacked and of expecting to be invited to share another's abundance in case of one's own need—that observers and historians, both native and foreigners, on the whole neglected even to mention it in their published accounts as an organizing principle of life. Caucasians, from the early explorers to modern-day tourists, have been overwhelmed by the spontaneous generosity of the Hawaiians, assuming commonly that this disposition was instinctively grounded—indeed, that it was a genetic weakness which they could not resist. Even Captain Cook, sensitive and understanding though he was, apparently failed to recognize the hospitality shown by the women for what it was intended:

The inhabitants . . . thronged off to the ship with hogs and women. It was not possible to keep the latter from coming on board and no women I ever met were less reserved. Indeed it appeared that they visited us with no other view than to make a surrender of their persons.[4]

Captain Cook, like so many of the later Western visitors, with their thorough indoctrination in the sanctity of private property, apparently interpreted the reciprocal aspects of hospitality as a 'propensity to thieving, which seems innate in most of the people we have visited in this ocean'.

At first on their entering the ship they endeavoured to steal everything they came near, or rather to take it openly, as what we either should not resent or not hinder. We soon convinced them of their mistake.[5]

[4] Cook, op. cit., p. 544.
[5] Ernest Rhys (ed.), *Captain Cook's Voyages of Discovery* (London, Everyman's Library, 1909), p. 331.

F

Other early visitors to the Islands were less disposed to question the morals of native hospitality, whether of sex or material goods, and were merely grateful in having encountered such good fortune as expressed, for example, by one of the officers of Captain Vancouver's crew in 1793:

> On the 7th, at sun rise the tababooiou (*kapu*) ceased. Joy and delight was ushered in with the new born day. In an instant our decks were covered with lovely women. Every Tar folded in his arms youth and beauty. . . . Pigs, cocoanuts and roots they offered without wishing for the least return; whilst the pretty Brunettes free from prudish ideas, led the way to the lonely Bowers and these yielded to our caresses without a thought of remuneration. After passing a few hours with these friendly people and partaking of an excellent dinner their liberality had provided us, we wished them farewell after having distributed some beads and other nicknacks amongst them.[6]

Missionary letters even in the latter half of the nineteenth century record something of the dismay and shock experienced by visiting Haole clergymen in the remote areas who were offered the hospitality of a daughter of the home as a companion for the night by a deacon of one of their churches.

Unfortunately most scholars of the Hawaiian social scene have failed to recognize that the social structure in which generosity and hospitality of this type are central and essential elements could in any way persist in the face of the assaults of a highly individualistic and competitive culture introduced from the West. One proposition of this nature has been repeated so frequently in scholarly accounts as to become almost axiomatic, namely that when the authoritative principle of *kapu*, assumed to be the key-stone supporting the Hawaiian social structure, was officially renounced by the King in 1819, the entire structure collapsed and nothing but the ruins of the old order remained. This widely used Polynesian term, *kapu*, *tapu*, or *tabu*, meaning to prohibit, restrict, or isolate by psychic authority because of either sanctity or defilement, applied to virtually every aspect of life in ancient Hawaii, and its undermining by constant

violations following 1778 seemed to spell the doom of everything Hawaiian. One ethnologist characterized the transformation as follows:

In the course of many centuries of complete isolation, the
native civilization had not only reached a condition of stability,
but was probably static. . . . Unquestionably the old culture was
ripe for its fall, like an apple gone beyond maturity on the tree.
Otherwise, the denouement could not have been so sudden and
so complete. The *kapu* in all of its ramifications and applications
had been carried to greater extremes than anywhere else in
Polynesia, until it had become a burden to chiefs, priests and
commoners alike.

Due to isolation, the Hawaiians were hungry for the stimulus
of new mores. They were primed for the headlong and disastrous
epoch of emulation of Euro-American mores into which, led by
their alii,[7] they plunged. . . . Kamehameha died in 1819. His
son, Liholiho, was inaugurated as *Moi* (king). Very shortly there-
after, as the result of a plan conceived and executed by the powerful chiefess, Kaahumanu (Kamehameha's favored consort),
Liholiho openly feasted with a company of both sexes, thereby
publicly proclaiming to a multitude of the common people
watching in amazement, the abolition of the *kapu*. As Alexander
writes: 'The effect of it was like that of displacing the keystone of
an arch. The whole structure both of idol-worship and of the
tabus fell at once into ruins.'[8]

W. H. R. Rivers, although impressed by Hawaii as 'the
most striking example of the permanence of social structure'
which he had met in the Pacific, nevertheless felt impelled
to state that 'there the original native culture is reduced to
the merest wreckage'.[9]

Studies of contemporary Hawaii reveal quite clearly,
however, that nothing quite so absolute or mechanistic as
the 'collapse of an arch' could have occurred and that many
of the traditional values of Hawaiian culture, sometimes in
disguised form, still persist and figure prominently in contemporary life. This is revealed most strikingly in the sharp

[7] *Alii* is the Hawaiian term referring to chiefs or persons in authority.

[8] E. S. Craighill Handy, *Cultural Revolution in Hawaii* (Honolulu, American
Council, Institute of Pacific Relations, 1931), p. 26.

[9] W. H. R. Rivers, 'The Ethnological Analysis of Culture', *Nature* (87,
1911), p. 359.

contrast between the Hawaiians and most of the immigrant groups with respect to the role of mutuality and reciprocity as controlling principles of life.

The peasant cultures from which immigrant labour groups to Hawaii were recruited shared with the folk peoples, such as the Hawaiians, much the same values of mutuality and of moral obligation to members of the in-group, commonly associated with a subsistence economy. But the peasant peoples of both Europe and Asia, who migrated to Hawaii, differed markedly from the folk in also having had prior experience with a trading economy in which gain is calculated and private property is highly valued. Most of Hawaii's people, by virtue of their peasant ancestry, whether recent as in the case of the Filipinos and Japanese, or more remote as among the Haoles, respond to a dual set of values—those of intimacy and fellow-feeling towards members of the in-group, contrasted with a striving for pecuniary advantage towards those outside the kinship and neighbourly bonds. It becomes increasingly difficult for all people to preserve any sort of equilibrium between conflicting forces in the face of mounting emphasis upon the latter set of values in an industrialized economy, but the immigrants and their children have at least the advantage of a tradition and some prior experience in relationships of that type.

In so far as there is any basis for characterizing the Hawaiians, ancient or modern, as a simple folk, it is a consequence of a life organization centred exclusively or predominantly around the principles appropriate to the family and primary-group relations. If the Hawaiians are unique among the peoples of Hawaii, it is in the fact that so many among them have refused to concern themselves with the task of combining and reconciling the conflicting roles of calculating tradesmen and obliging kinsmen. Many Hawaiians— more than in most of Hawaii's ethnic groups—are 'peculiar' in retaining so tenaciously the dispositions engendered universally in small face-to-face groups of entering imaginatively into the experiences of others and so discouraging in themselves the disposition to exploit and manipulate. This, briefly stated, is the Hawaiian's unique contribution to

Hawaii's amicable race relations and at the same time the basis of his failure as a competitor in the present-day struggle.

This apparent paradox is further amplified in a set of observations by Romanzo Adams in the early 1930s, which relates, however, exclusively to that segment of the Hawaiian community which had almost completely retained the traditional expectations and obligations:

Commonly they do not feel that it is important to keep on working when they have enough for the near future. They are willing to work some of the time for a living, but they want to take some time to live—some time for activities that are valued for their own sake. These enjoyable activities are not postponed to old age nor until one has acquired wealth. A man takes his enjoyment as he goes, even at the risk of not being financially prepared for an emergency.

To an old-fashioned Hawaiian, the practices of the hard-boiled business man are immoral. One would be ashamed to drive a hard bargain based on another man's necessity, to refuse credit to a man in need merely because payment is improbable, to embarrass a debtor by urging payment, or to avow so much interest in making money or in keeping it when others are in need. Commonly an Hawaiian man cannot make even a start toward economic competence because if he accumulates some property his moral standards compel him to share it with his needy relatives and friends. They 'eat him out'. Occasionally there is the exception that proves the rule. . . . An Hawaiian man . . . was helping them [a group of Hawaiians] to acquire larger incomes than they had known before, but he lost his position as leader. He urged the men to work too much of the time and they thought he was grasping. His conduct was not determined by motives that were respectable from the standpoint of the old moral order.[10]

MUTUALITY AND THE ALOHA SPIRIT IN A CHANGING WORLD

The failure of Caucasians generally to recognize survival of the traditional Hawaiian moral order has by no means made them oblivious to a distinct Hawaiian character or tempera-

[10] Romanzo Adams, *Interracial Marriage in Hawaii* (New York, Macmillan Co., 1938), p. 244.

ment supposedly innately acquired. The early European and American visitors from the exploring and trading vessels found it convenient to interpret the hospitality they enjoyed among the natives as instinctively grounded and hence demanding neither restraint nor reciprocity on their part. The missionaries tended to view Hawaiian permissiveness with respect to sex and property as evidence of 'the basest of human passions', actually of the animal nature in man. Hopefully by the grace of God, however, even people so 'ignorant, debased, and wedded to their sins' might be recreated into the new persons of which their essential kindliness and sympathy gave some promise. The planters, on the other hand, with their concern for a permanent and reliable labour force, were chiefly impressed by the 'indolence, inconstancy and improvidence' of the Hawaiians.

In the accounts by Caucasians about Hawaii throughout the century following discovery there were references to the good nature and friendliness of the natives: Captain Cook led the long array of those extolling the virtues of the Islanders, with the following comments made at the close of his first month of contacts with them:

They seem to be blest with a frank, cheerful disposition; they live very sociably with one another, and, except for the propensity to thieving, which seems innate in most of the people we have visited in this ocean, they were exceedingly friendly to us. It was a pleasure to observe with how much affection the women manage their infants, and how readily the men lent their assistance to such a tender office, thus distinguishing themselves from those savages who esteem a wife and child as things rather necessary than desirable, or worthy of their notice.[11]

The missionaries in general were considerably more restrained in their commendations of Hawaiian character, since their function in Hawaii had been partially conceived to root out the evils from an unenlightened people. They did, however, refer repeatedly to being greeted by 'countenances beaming with love', 'their childish exclamations of

[11] Rhys, op. cit., p. 337.

delight', and the great quantities of gifts, especially of native food, which they received, in return for which they were expected 'to shake hands and repeat *aloha*'.[12] The unwillingness of the natives to submit to the monotony and drudgery of the plantation regimen resulted in their continued characterization on that frontier as 'lazy, and undependable', and yet many of the planters were glad to hire them whenever they were available because of their 'cheerful dispositions, good humor, and skill in handling animals'.

Under the impact of the varied external forces, outlined earlier, the great majority of the Hawaiians tended to absorb much of the material culture of the West, without necessarily being divested of their own traditional moral values.[13] With a population as large and as variously situated as the Hawaiians, the assimilation of the more basic and critical values of foreign cultures has proceeded quite unevenly. In general, those of unmixed Hawaiian ancestry or who have continued to live in the more remote, isolated and least commercially desirable regions of the Islands have retained more of the traditional Hawaiian ways of life and have likewise encountered more of the problems of culture conflict. The remainder of this chapter is chiefly concerned with this portion of the more than 100,000 Hawaiians and part-Hawaiians—a minority, however, whose number and influence vary with the situation involved and continue to decline in importance with the passage of time.

The use of the term *aloha* as an adjective relating specifically to the outgoing and generous dispositions among the Hawaiians appears to have emerged on the tourist frontier and to have been propagated most widely within the tourist community. As a salutation or greeting, expressing goodwill or pleasure towards either stranger or kinsman, the word

[12] Laura Fish Judd, *Honolulu: Sketches of the Life, Social, Political, and Religious, in the Hawaiian Islands from 1828 to 1861* (New York, Anson D. F. Randolph and Co., 1880).

[13] The acculturation process as relating to the Hawaiians is too involved for presentation here. Important aspects have been discussed in Edwin G. Burrows, *Hawaiian Americans* (Yale University Press, 1947), Ernest Beaglehole, *Some Modern Hawaiians* (University of Hawaii Press, 1937), and Andrew W. Lind, 'Some Modifications of Hawaiian Character', in E. B. Reuter, op. cit.

aloha had its counterpart among most of the island peoples of
the Pacific and had been widely employed in intercourse
between natives and foreigners in Hawaii from the early
nineteenth century onwards. As a description of a way of life
which is peculiarly Hawaiian and reflects a dominating
disposition of friendliness and generosity towards one's fellows,
the term aloha spirit has gained wide currency in the community only within the post-war era, partly as a useful
adjunct of the tourist industry. It is significant that neither
Beaglehole nor Burrows, the two anthropologists whose
publications on the Hawaiians appeared during the 1930s
and 1940s, made any direct reference to aloha or the aloha
spirit in their own analyses and included the terms only as
used by their informants. On the other hand, both Handy
and Emory, whose services as ethnologist and anthropolo-
gist at the Bishop Museum extended back to 1920, evidently
conceived of it as central in the legacy from the Hawaiians to
all the people of Hawaii.[14]

Newspaper editorials and feature articles, with such titles
as 'What is the Aloha Spirit?', 'Strains on Aloha Spirit',
'Russians Conquered Aloha Spirit', 'Aloha: Fact and Fiction', testify to the widespread recognition and diverse interpretations of a set of dispositions among the Hawaiians so
deeply rooted as to appear instinctive and so powerful as to
pervade the entire social atmosphere of the Islands. One of
the most prominent Hawaiian clergymen, in a community-
wide Thanksgiving address on the occasion of the granting
of statehood to Hawaii, went so far as to endow the aloha
spirit with divine qualities.

Aloha is the power of God seeking to unite what is separated
in the world—the power that unites heart with heart, . . . race
with race. . . . Thus when a people live in the spirit of aloha, they
live in the spirit of God. . . . A person who has the spirit of aloha
loves even when the love is not returned, and such is the love of
God. This is the meaning of aloha.[15]

[14] E. S. Craighill Handy, Kenneth P. Emory and others, *Ancient Hawaiian
Civilization* (Rutland, Vermont, Charles E. Tuttle Co., 1965), pp. 20, 312.
[15] Abraham K. Akaka, Sermon delivered at Thanksgiving Service at
Kawaiahao Church, Honolulu (13 March 1959).

In so far as aloha is a quality found universally in primary-group experiences by which man acquires the capacities that are thought to be most truly human—of entering imaginatively into the experience of others and thus learning to be compassionate, sensitive, and loving—there is justification for such sanctification.

Like other idealized qualities, questions immediately arise as to how genuine and authentic the expressions of aloha really are, how widely they are observed, and the extent to which they are exploited as means to less worthy ends. The temptation to make use of such childlike qualities as those inherent in the aloha of the Hawaiians has been especially pronounced under the highly competitive conditions of the modern tourist world. The extensive employment of persons of Hawaiian ancestry in the tourist trade as entertainers and tour guides, presumably because of the 'spontaneity of their aloha' and their cheerful, relaxing dispositions, has been interpreted by critics as the 'exploitation of children and the deception of gullible tourists by the tales and antics of children'. No special insight is required to discover that even the 'easy-going and happy-go-lucky' Hawaiians may become irritated and tense under provocation—that aloha may evaporate and give place to anger or worse.

Old-timers also contend that the spirit of spontaneous hospitality is less prevalent among Hawaiians in the 1960s than it was in the 1930s and less today in the cities than in the remote rural areas. When in addition the theory is advanced that the Hawaiians have succeeded, presumably by some sort of social osmosis, to transmit their outgoing and loving dispositions to all the permanent residents of the Islands, the conclusion quickly reached by some is that aloha is chiefly a gimmick for tourists. The Hawaiians themselves recognize the manner in which their heritage has sometimes been appropriated for commercial purposes:

Nowadays, many people lament the fact that the aloha spirit is being exploited by businessmen and politicians. Our tourist literature is plastered with aloha, the HVB (Hawaii Visitors Bureau) constantly trumpets the need for more and more aloha, the Chamber of Commerce urges its perpetuation through the schools. . . . But lest we forget, tourism still brings in millions of dollars for thousands of Island residents.

Our politicians propagandize the same monotonous message —Hawaii is the Aloha state—in Washington, Athens or Tokyo, wherever their junkets take them, 'Hawaii is the melting pot where East and West meet in a truly harmonious multi-ethnic society, a marvelous example for the rest of the world to emulate.' Unconsciously, so it seems, we are building our own state ideology. To be sure, this is myth-making, but I suppose this is the stuff of which realities are made, too. The aloha spirit, after all, is both fact and fiction.[16]

Data derived from essays written by a broad cross-section of University of Hawaii students on the topic 'What the Aloha Spirit Means to Me' reveal a great diversity of meanings attached to the term. At the one extreme is the cynical definition of the disillusioned tourist student, with the caption, 'For Sale—Aloha Spirit':

The amount of the Aloha Spirit which the tourist takes back with him is, in most cases directly proportional to the amount of money which he has to spend. . . . In the commercial setting of Waikiki where thousands of tourists flock each year, the Aloha Spirit is distributed much like S & H Green Stamps—the more you buy and the greater amount you spend, the more you get in return. Tip the beachboy a little more than usual and he may tell you some interesting surfing stories, buy two orchids instead of one at the corner flower stand, and the kindness of the local proprietor will be overwhelming. Step right up and buy your Aloha Spirit, because it can be purchased anywhere in Waikiki, and in some cases, the results are most satisfying. The itinerary of the tourist may suitably end with the phrase, 'Aloha Spirit, slight extra charge.'

Among the total of sixty-two Island and Mainland advanced students who participated in the inquiry, there were three who seemed convinced that the aloha spirit was merely a tourist trap, although a good many others recognized that the tourist industry capitalized on the idea.

With these exceptions, all the students, both local and

[16] George S. Kanahele, 'Aloha: Fact and Fiction', *Honolulu Advertiser* (30 January 1968).

Mainland, conceived of the aloha spirit as a genuine and authentic quality of the behaviour among Islanders, notably among the Hawaiians, in which warmth of feeling and a disposition to be helpful were quite spontaneous and unaffected. Repeatedly the Hawaiians were represented as deriving special pleasure from sharing whatever they had with others without any concern for compensation. Other student informants were equally insistent that the same atmosphere of mutual helpfulness was just as natural and spontaneous within the other ethnic groups. In certain groups, such as the Japanese, this subjective sense of satisfaction from sharing has also been greatly re-enforced by the pressure of the moral order, by which the individual is constantly made aware of the obligation to share.

By way of summary, there can be no question as to the well-grounded tradition of hospitality and mutual aid in Hawaiian culture nor of its persistence to a marked degree down to the present day, although the changed conditions of life now do threaten its future course to some degree. Ironically, the survival of the aloha spirit—the aspect of Hawaiian culture which is most highly lauded by the Western world—is nevertheless the source of major difficulties encountered by Hawaiians in their adjustment to the civilization now evolving in these islands.

THE HAWAIIAN DILEMMA

To the casual observer it might appear that the social adjustments required of the Hawaiian were not essentially different from those faced by the various immigrant groups—the necessity of choosing among the elements of their traditional and adoptive cultures to make their own or to reject. For the native people, however, the problem is presented quite differently than for those arriving from another land, to whom the contrast between the old and the new can be readily and sharply defined. For the indigenes, the old and the new fuse imperceptibly, and it becomes increasingly difficult to differentiate between the traditional and the contemporary. To the children of the land—and eventually this becomes true also of the descendants of the immigrants—the only clear distinction becomes one of time and disposition between their 'old-fashioned' parents and themselves. Their failure to recognize the extent to which their own desires and expectations have been influenced by the ancestral values of the dim, distant past testifies further to the unconscious depth—the level of the mores—at which these controls operate. The fact that Hawaiian culture has long since ceased to provide an adequate basis for life organization does not detract, however, from the significant part which these vestiges may still play in the life of the community.

One of the notable developments of the present generation of Hawaiians has been a reawakening of interest on the part of a few in what they conceive to be their racial heritage. How to reconcile the dominant emphasis on the 'success psychology' of the West with the central values of mutuality and sharing in the Hawaiian tradition is, however, a dilemma to which no satisfactory solution has yet been found. The acceptance of the basic values of the traditional culture is to entail disfavour from the larger community for violating its canons, whereas conformity to these canons involves an inevitable loss of self- and communal integrity. Although it may be said that variants of this dilemma underlie many, if not all, of the major problems of a rapidly changing society, it assumes more dramatic proportions for the Hawaiians because of the decided difference in the values involved. For the immigrant peasants and their children, the prior experience within a trading economy and the incorporation of some of its requirements within the traditional culture made the tension between the old and the new far less acute.

The history of the Hawaiians over the nearly two centuries which have elapsed since discovery by the West reflects both the survival of vestigial aspects of the ancient culture and some of the difficulties resulting from their retention. The very rapid adoption by the natives of certain aspects of Western culture and civilization, such as literacy, the external forms of the Christian religion, and much of the material and technological aspects of a capitalistic civiliza-

tion, led to the mistaken notion that the indigenous culture
has been completely wiped out and that all Hawaiians had
become Europeans or American Islanders.

As indicated in the earlier portions of this chapter, however, much of the basic core of the Hawaiian moral order
withstood the impact of the West, and many of the central
values have continued to function to the present in but thinly
disguised form. During the peak of their success in converting
the natives during the 1830s, the missionaries became aware
of 'much hypocrisy among the people and not a little wicked-
ness in secret', and even ten years later it was reported that
'of our adult church members we can hardly say there are
any who have so put off their former heathenish habits and
acquired such an amount of intelligence, prudence, and
maturity of Christian character as to justify an attempt to
train them to be pastors and teachers of our churches'.[17]

The tragic decline of the Hawaiian population, threaten-
ing its extinction by the end of the century, the passing of
much of their land to white invaders, the encounter with
alien peoples who came as labourers but soon surpassed them
in the economic struggle, and the final collapse of the native
monarchy, their one remaining symbol of position and power
in their own land—these successively engendered a distaste
for what the foreigners had brought and a desire among
many to return to their ancient ways. A variety of nativistic
movements, including several armed rebellions and a number of esoteric religious cults, appeared during the last
quarter of the nineteenth century, and the latter have continued throughout the present century to reflect some of the
native aversion towards Western values, and their own
efforts to reconstruct and preserve the old. Fraternal and
civic organizations and lodges, confined to persons of
Hawaiian ancestry and requiring in some as a condition of
membership a genealogy of chiefly rank, have given added
support to the ethnic values which still persist.

Far more pervasive in its influence has been the unconscious retention by many Hawaiians of a complex of customs,
practices, and beliefs derived from their kinship and com-

[17] *Missionary Herald* (no. 38, 1842), p. 471.

munity surroundings, of whose very existence they may be quite unaware. This is especially notable in the areas where the ratio of full Hawaiians to part-Hawaiians and of all persons of Hawaiian ancestry to the total population is high. Curiously enough, some of the most striking instances of this type of ethnic residential segregation in Hawaii are the result of legislation by the Congress of the United States, sponsored by the Hawaiian delegate, Prince Kalanianaole, and intended, of course, for the special benefit of persons of Hawaiian ancestry. The Hawaiian Rehabilitation Bill of 1920 provided that persons with 50 per cent or more of Hawaiian blood might apply for a homestead—actually a 99-year lease—at the insignificant cost of one dollar per year. The consequence has been the creation on all the major islands, but especially in Honolulu or its vicinity, of a number of semi-segregated communities in which the owner of every leasehold is Hawaiian, although other members of the household may be non-Hawaiian. As one would expect, it is in these officially constituted communities and the very small isolated and remote communities on the outer islands, consisting predominantly of Hawaiians and part-Hawaiians, where the aloha spirit appears to be best preserved and, by the same token, their difficulties of adjustment to the requirements of the Western world are also most acute.

A recently conducted study in the remote portions of the district of Kona on the island of Hawaii illustrates somewhat further the nature of this paradox. The district of Kona covers an area of more than 800 square miles, much of which consists only of the barren lava flows extending down to the sea from two major volcanic peaks within or adjacent to the district. The Hawaiians, especially those of pure native stock, have constituted a disproportionate part of the total population throughout the period for which census data are available, and many of them live in isolated fishing villages along the coast or in remote ranching and semi-subsistence hamlets at a higher elevation, but avoided by residents of other ethnic groups because of the meagre opportunities for gaining a livelihood.

The Western economy has only partially taken hold

among the Hawaiians in these areas, and the Western empha-
ses upon individual initiative and striving are also less evident. Instead, the principles of communal sharing, appropriate to a folk culture, tend to predominate, and the individual
who is grasping and self-seeking, or 'ambitious' in the
Western sense, simply does not find this a congenial atmosphere in which to live. On the other hand, those who cannot
adjust to the competitive struggle and the mechanized mode
of living in the world outside find in the remote areas of
Kona a satisfactory haven.

Despite the very meagre financial income derived from a
quasi-subsistence economy, the disposition of the Hawaiian
residents to share what they have—a catch of fish, for example—with visitors from outside becomes frequently an
embarrassment to those accustomed to the individualistic
and property-minded striving in Western society.

An inevitable corollary of the tendency to withdraw from
the competitive struggle in the world outside is the disposition to look to the State, as the present-day successor of the
ancient *alii*, to share its wealth among those less fortunately
situated. A marked disproportion of the financial and personal assistance from the State Public Welfare Department
goes to households from the predominantly Hawaiian communities, where the very low average monetary incomes are
further dissipated by Hawaiian hospitality. The problems in
such communities sometimes become hopelessly complicated
between the American standards of private property,
individual enterprise, and foresight in budgetary planning, on
the one hand, and the Hawaiian traditions of generosity,
especially as they relate to property and sex, on the other
hand. The social workers, bound by the legal requirement
of strict accountability for the funds they authorize, face the
embarrassing and well-nigh impossible task of interpreting
to their clients why additional funds are not forthcoming
when the monthly allotment has been prematurely exhausted
in sharing with visiting kinfolk and friends. The preference
of these Hawaiians for employment of a casual and sporadic
nature such as fishing, when the spirit moves, or working for
a few days a week in picking coffee or working on the country

roads, but of avoiding occupations requiring continuous service at regular hours, has led, of course, to the common stereotypes of their being 'lazy, lacking in ambition and industry, and improvident'.

The casual and permissive attitudes towards pre-marital and extra-marital sex and towards common-law marriage and illegitimacy encountered among the Hawaiians in these communities may be interpreted by a few knowledgeable social workers as the natural expression of their traditional values, specifically of the aloha spirit. Unfortunately for the Hawaiians, however, according to the legal code enforced by the State and the sanctions of important guardians of public esteem like the school and the Church, such behaviour is still generally defined as immoral, if not criminal. Closely associated with the freedom and liberality in sex relations is the shifting and unpredictable nature of the household composition. It is not uncommon for a Hawaiian household in Kona to consist of an elderly couple and several nieces and nephews, some of whom are 'borrowed for a while', or of an aged matriarch and the children of her unmarried sons or daughters, the parents of whom may drift in and out of the home from time to time. Social case records from the district reveal the common practice of the *hanai* in which a child is given away at birth to relatives or friends 'to feed' and nurture, a practice frequently leading to serious difficulties in the application of Western conceptions of legal and moral responsibility.

The potential complications resulting from the lack of firmly established ties between the generations can be readily imagined. The likelihood of influencing children to accept and adhere to the definitions of appropriate conduct by outside agencies such as the law, the school, or the Church is obviously less if the influence of the parental generation is widely scattered among numerous persons, most of whom are not themselves deeply committed to such conventional values. Children of Hawaiian ancestry, especially from the more remote communities, have acquired a lasting reputation with school authorities for their minimal motivation in academic pursuits, the frequency of their absences or with-

drawal from school, their undisciplined conduct, and disregard for 'the sanctity of private property and sex'.

Comparable situations have developed elsewhere within
the Islands, wherever considerable numbers of Hawaiians
have been drawn together in communities chiefly of their
own, such as the homestead areas under Governmental
auspices, the rural retreats like Kona, or the ghettos of Oahu
and Honolulu. These are commonly areas of low average
incomes—the poverty areas, where competition and personal striving are weak, and manifestations of the aloha
spirit and mutuality are strong. This condition, however, is
pervasive enough to support such contrasting stereotypes of
Hawaiians in the mass as 'happy-go-lucky, lazy, spend all of
their money at once, take and give things freely never thinking whether they need them or not, easy to get along with,
although violent when angry, real hard workers if they love
their job, immoral, sweet and friendly'.[18]

The composite record of the Hawaiians, judged by Western criteria, is similarly ambivalent. The proportion of
illegitimate births, for example, has been roughly twice as
high among the Hawaiians during the 1960s as in the entire
population of the State, and among the full Hawaiians it has
been between three to four times as high as among the part-
Hawaiians. Similarly recent studies of juvenile and adult
delinquency, as defined by Western law, indicate a wholly
disproportionate share originating among the Hawaiians. In
the early 1960s, 45 per cent of all children under the care of
the Honolulu Juvenile Court were Hawaiians, most of the
boys for crimes against property and the girls for sex offences.
Just a few years later (1964), 57 per cent of all the male
inmates and 48 per cent of the female inmates from the
entire State at the Youth Correctional Facilities were of
Hawaiian ancestry, whereas all the Hawaiian youngsters of
a comparable age constituted only 21 per cent of the total
population. At about the same time, 42 per cent of the adult
inmates of Hawaii's Correctional Facilities were of Hawaiian
ancestry, which was more than three times the Hawaiian

[18] 'Characterization of Hawaiians by Non-Hawaiian Students' (University
of Hawaii, 1952).

G

proportion of the adult population. Of the Hawaiian juveniles, at least, it might be said that an important contributing factor to the 'delinquency' among the girls was the fact of their manifesting too much of the aloha spirit, whereas in the cases of the boys the difficulty was that they took the hospitality and generosity among others too much for granted.[19] The records reveal, on the other hand, that the rate of mental breakdown, as measured by the admissions to the State Hospital, is singularly low among Hawaiians, as compared with other ethnic groups.[20] It has been suggested that the Hawaiians tend to act out their aggressions rather than to turn them inwards. Similarly their suicide rate is low.

This aspect of the Hawaiian dilemma might be stated in summary as a conflict growing out of contact with the foreigners and their civilization. The Hawaiian aloha, with its hospitality and generosity towards both kinfolk and strangers, so greatly extolled as a 'Christian virtue' to be preserved and encouraged, is the basis for reproof and punishment when applied too freely with respect to private property and sex. Western civilization as a whole, of course, reflects the same inherent ambiguity between its peasant tradition of mutual aid and helpfulness and the competitive and individualistic incentives which modern mass society has so greatly intensified.

It would, of course, be quite inaccurate to suggest that Hawaiians as a whole have retained any considerable portion of the cultural traditions which are subject to such adverse interpretations in the light of Western values. Even among the minority nurtured in a supposedly Hawaiian tradition and atmosphere, it must be recognized that a fully integrated indigenous culture as basis for individual life organization has long since ceased to exist. Scattered vestiges

[19] This interpretation of the highly disproportionate ratios of so-called 'criminal behaviour' among Hawaiians does not discount the operation of other factors, such as the development of a complex of practices and customs during childhood and adolescence which are defined by the wider community as antisocial and which may continue into adulthood.

[20] Bernhard Hormann, 'Native Welfare in Hawaii', *Proceedings of the Seventh Pacific Science Congress* (Auckland, 1953), p. 89.

alone remain, but these are sometimes important enough to colour notably the relationships across racial lines. The great majority of Hawaiians, both adults and children, have absorbed as their own the expectations and goals of contemporary Western society, and are subject to much the same tensions and uncertainties with respect to conflicting objectives. In so far as marked deviations in conduct from Western standards do occur, especially in the heavily weighted Hawaiian communities, the evidence frequently points to the survival of practices which are quite 'moral' from the perspective of the indigenous culture.

The other facet of the Hawaiian dilemma, less involved perhaps but no less a matter of concern to students of race relations, bears upon the supposed loss of any distinctive ethnic heritage by so many members of this large minority of the Island population. With a mounting proportion each year of persons with only a fraction of Polynesian blood in their veins, the probability of their preserving authentic Hawaiian traditions and culture seems likely to diminish and the sense of what is Hawaiian tends to become less and less distinct. Quite understandably many of those who retain a consciousness of themselves as Hawaiians, regardless of their other group identifications, feel a distinct loss in self-esteem as a result of what they see happening to them.

The history of the nineteenth and twentieth centuries in their total impact, it must be granted, has not been conducive to the building or the preservation of any high degree of group pride on the part of the native Hawaiians. The tragic decline in numbers throughout the first 120 years of contact, seeming to foretoken the eventual and certain extinction of the race, brought on among the more thoughtful members a depression of spirit which even their natural exuberance and optimism could not wholly counteract. Nor had the parallel development among the other ethnic groups, especially the Haoles, of a tendency persisting down to the present of referring to the Hawaiians as a 'dying race', helped at all to allay this loss of confidence.

Another important source of increasing despondency was the loss by many Hawaiians at a fairly early date of title to their lands—their one certain source of livelihood. The vigorous pressure during the first half of the nineteenth century by American and European settlers resulted in the individualization of land titles in Hawaii at a much earlier date (1846) than elsewhere in the Pacific and at a time when the natives were wholly unprepared to deal with land in terms of buying and selling. The discovery by the close of the century that the ownership and control of most of the best agricultural lands had shifted into the hands of Caucasians through a system of alienation legalized by a native administration only intensified their dismay at having been victimized by those they had befriended.

The overthrow of the Hawaiian monarchy by Americans and Europeans in 1893 and the annexation of the Islands by the United States in 1898 seemed to many the death blow to native pride and self-esteem, and the open and widespread weeping at the ceremonies on 4 July 1898, when the Hawaiian flag was lowered for the last time, testified to the even wider sense of alienation by those who would not attend what must have seemed a public flaunting of their collective humiliation.

Annexation did, however, bring with it certain temporary gains in status to the Hawaiians through the granting of full citizenship and voting rights to all persons born in Hawaii. Owing to the exclusion from such privileges of the large proportion of immigrant labourers, the Hawaiians, who constituted only 15 per cent of the adult population at the time of annexation, controlled 69 per cent of the vote in Territorial elections. Had they been disposed to vote as a bloc, they could have dictated for a period of over two decades much of the Island legislation, and by the sheer dominance in the number of their voters Hawaiians did constitute the largest number of elected officials for well over two decades. This advantage, however, was gradually lost as the proportion of Island-born persons of Oriental ancestry increased such that by 1940, the last date for which such data were compiled, the Hawaiians constituted only 25 per cent of the voters. Since the war that proportion has doubtless dropped to little more than 15 per cent. The loss of the political advantage once held by the Hawaiians was not any easier to bear from the realization that their earlier preferred position had been at the expense of others less fortunate. The significant resistance among Hawaiians to Statehood reflected in large part a blind fear that such a radical change in Governmental structure could only mean a further decline in their political power and the possible removal of the few perquisites within the State which they still retained.

There were actually relatively few special privileges or cultural traditions also highly valued in the Western world which the Hawaiians could claim to be uniquely their own, and this fact explains in part the extreme tenacity with which some Hawaiians have sought to preserve these few. Despite the small number of families benefiting as home-steaders under the Hawaiian Homes Commission Act— a mere 1,752 in 1964—and the questionable advantage which was thereby provided, no political figure with any expectation of continued widespread support in the community would think of questioning publicly the retention of this provision in the new State constitution.

Part of the aura of sanctity which has developed around the preservation of the Hawaiian Homes Commission of course grows out of the widespread attitude of pathos towards the Hawaiians, especially within the Haole community, the sense that, however innocently it has occurred, the indigenous peoples of these Islands, like the Indians on the U.S. Mainland, have been victimized and exploited by the invaders. It was seriously argued by one prominent Island author, for example, that 'of all the Polynesian islands, only the Hawaiians were stripped of their lands with no attempt made to protect them', and 'control of the Homes lands by Congress has been the only safeguard for Hawaiians in the past. Take that away and they would again be left landless in the home of their forefathers'.[21]

Similarly the sentiment which has been aroused within the Hawaiian community, as well as outside among certain

[21] Kathleen D. Mellen, 'Letter to the Editor', *Honolulu Star-Bulletin* (22 March 1968).

Haoles, in support of the policies of the largest estate in the Islands is made to appear as a valiant effort to safeguard one of the last embattled strongholds of Hawaiian rights. The B. P. Bishop Estate, which controls slightly over 9 per cent of the total land area of the State, was established under provisions of the will of Princess Bernice Pauahi Bishop, the last survivor of the Kamehameha line of Hawaiian royalty, to provide for 'the education of the children of Hawaii'. This has been interpreted by the predominantly Haole trustees of the Bishop Estate as applying to children of Hawaiian ancestry, and consequently the Kamehameha Schools, established by the Estate and with one of the largest endowments of any school in the United States, has come to be conceived by some as a special commitment to the Hawaiians which they are obligated to protect from any possible attack. Actually only a small proportion of the children of Hawaiian ancestry, less than one-tenth of those of school age, are able to benefit from the special facilities of the Kamehameha Schools, but their existence nevertheless symbolizes for the Hawaiians one asset of unquestioned value in the larger Western community which is peculiarly and exclusively theirs.

Proposed legislation to enable a larger proportion of the population to own land and requiring the large land-holders, such as the Bishop Estate, to sell portions of their land under certain circumstances has been very vigorously resisted by some of the Hawaiians as a further attack upon them and their waning rights. It is not evident to most non-Hawaiians how such legislation would necessarily affect adversely the financial strength of the Bishop Estate, much less how it would threaten the position of the Hawaiians as a whole, but so great is the sensitivity to further encroachments from any possible source that public demonstrations and organized movements have developed among them by way of protest.

An institution of such outstanding wealth whose benefits are confined exclusively to members of a single ethnic group quite naturally has come under criticism as being racially discriminatory, especially in a community which has emphasized its general freedom from such practices, and the question has been publicly raised repeatedly as to whether the trustees of the Bishop Estate are either morally or legally justified in restricting enrolment in the Kamehameha Schools to children of Hawaiian ancestry. The minister of the largest Hawaiian church in the Islands and one of the principal spokesmen for those who seek to revive a sense of ethnic pride among the Hawaiians, has seized upon this and the correlated land reform issues as a symbol around which to rally the scattered forces of a twentieth-century nativistic movement:

And there are those who would take away this means of our uplift and open our schools to other races. As long as there is one needy Hawaiian child who needs to get into Kamehameha, he or she should not be bypassed for any other. It is the will of our Princess that 'preference shall be given to the children of full or part aboriginal blood'.

Our native people have already given away or lost much of their possessions. The time comes when a people need to say, 'This much and no more.' Because of the need for courageous defense . . . the Friends of Kamehameha Schools came into being.[22]

Probably the time has passed when one could expect to generate substantial support for such an 'Operation Hawaiian Uplift', conceived as a means either to 'perpetuate Hawaiian language, culture, and arts', as a resolution recently proposed in the State Legislature, or to revive among the Hawaiians generally a sense of pride in their ancestral heritage.

Quite an opposite point of view is more commonly held in the wider community of Hawaii, partially expressed in an editorial directed towards the legislative proposal and entitled, 'Clinging to a Lost Culture':

. . . We do not think they [legislators] seriously believe that the Hawaiian language is of any practical importance to anyone save Hawaiian scholars or songwriters in the year 1968. Indeed, most of today's 'Hawaiian' songs are written in English—or pidgin. The ancient language has even lost its political significance and

[22] *Honolulu Advertiser* (15 September 1967).

has appeared on election notices and ballots in recent years merely as a quaint but harmless anachronism . . . there are better ways to use the limited time of our . . . pupils than trying to make Hawaiian scholars of them or to keep alive a culture that could not survive on its own in contemporary civilization.[23]

One of the more vocal, if not the most highly regarded, spokesmen in the Hawaiian community, urges what constitutes in reality a renunciation of any special reserves or privileges for his fellows simply because they are Hawaiians:

I have never really approved of the Hawaiian Homes Commission nor of the basic concepts and philosophy that underlie its founding. It seems to smack too much of paternalism, or protectionism, of dependency upon the government for survival instead of one's own self. . . . To the ordinary Hawaiian, too much protection could well spell disaster for he must survive, not in the Eden that most romanticists have painted, . . . but in a highly competitive social structure that hourly becomes more complex. Nor can the Hawaiian, in dreams of an improbable past, withdraw from the rough give and take of everyday living. He must participate and . . . compete. Else he will surely become a museum piece.[24]

The fact that this was written from inside a prison does not detract from its relevance or authenticity.

A more moderate point of view, avoiding both extremes of an uncritical adulation of a 'lost culture' on the one hand or its complete rejection on the other, in favour of a complete absorption within the individualistic and competitive atmosphere of the West, probably reflects the temper of most present-day Hawaiians. Pride in the tradition of generosity and tolerance from their aboriginal forebears—a tradition that refuses to condemn people for their infractions of conventional Western moral codes—is apparently not wholly inconsonant with the satisfactions derived from the use of their talents 'in all areas of present-day life, as active, participating, productive, first-class citizens of the United States'. The frank admission that 'many of us are in jails and corrective institutions . . . on public welfare rolls . . . on the

[23] *Honolulu Star-Bulletin* (22 March 1968).
[24] *Honolulu Advertiser* (9 April 1968).

lowest rung of the social and economic ladder . . . in a sad plight . . . in the prosperous land of our progenitors' can be faced with an equally honest recognition that 'many of us have found places in every area of Island life . . . among the educators, artists, architects, clergymen, lawyers, physicians and businessmen and political leaders of the State'.[25] All things considered, perhaps the Hawaiians who are frankly and openly Hawaiian in their outlook are less schizoid and less at odds with themselves than the majority of Hawaii's residents who are so frequently torn between a driving ambition for 'success' in the competitive struggle, on the one hand, and the unconscious urging to be humane, on the other.

[25] John Dominis Holt, *On Being Hawaiian* (Honolulu, 1964), pp. 25-6.

V | Prospects

What are the net results of nearly two centuries of inter-racial contact in Hawaii and what may be expected for the future in a region of such rapid social change? These are questions which are being asked with increasing frequency and uncertainty by knowledgeable observers who only a few years ago would have had ready and positive answers to any such queries by outsiders. Developments since World War II and especially following statehood have greatly intensified the number and diversity of contacts with the outside world, and the city and county of Honolulu, embracing as it does over 80 per cent of the entire population of the State, has assumed more and more the character of a metropolis along what Robert E. Park has termed the 'Main Street of the World'. Thus the overwhelming proportion of Hawaii's people are immersed in a social environment somewhat comparable in terms of the impersonality of life and the rapidity of social change to that of Singapore, Hong Kong, Los Angeles, New York, London, or Paris, and some observers contend therefore that Honolulu is vulnerable to the same dangers of class and racial convulsions to which these larger centres have been subjected in recent years.

RACIAL PRIDE AND PREJUDICE

There are, in fact, two contrasting types of racial disharmony from which Hawaii might conceivably be threatened. The one most commonly thought to exist is the emergence of a pride of ancestry comparable to that of Black Power which has seemed so ominous to satisfactory race relations in

continental United States in recent years. Kamaaina clergymen, visiting journalists, and even some social scientists
profess to see in some of the recent ethnic developments in
Hawaii the ingredients of a potentially serious outburst of
racial feelings. An Island-born Episcopal minister, with
prior experience as a journalist in Hawaii, while conceding
that 'all of us who live here and love these islands know that
we have a degree of love and acceptance that is the envy of
the whole world', went on to express regret regarding the
many racially oriented groups in the community as contributing to a 'ghetto mentality' expressed in the 'blasphemous
conclusion that "nobody loves us but ourselves".'

In Hawaii, we have a long history of racially oriented social or
business or political pressure groups—the Japanese Chamber of
Commerce, the Chinese societies, the Filipino Federation of
America, and the Pacific Club, to mention a few. I believe that
any organization that segregates because of race is wrong in its
admission policies, however its members may crow about 'freedom of choice'. Such organizations foster a type of ghetto
authority. . . . The Hawaiian Civic Clubs, the Kaahumanu
Society, the Kamehameha Alumni Association all had in the
beginning and still have as their noble aim the welfare of the
Hawaiian people. . . . The trouble is that while they are saying
'let us help the unfortunate of our race,' the unfortunate of the
race are being taught . . . that the battle of Modern Hawaii is in
reality a battle between themselves and the rest of the world.[1]

This, of course, is a re-echoing in contemporary terms of
the earlier criticisms of any organized movements, including
foreign-language schools and mutual-aid societies, especially
among the immigrant groups, as constituting a potential
subversion of established authority and as an obstacle to
effective and rapid assimilation. The further implication
deduced in the light of present-day developments elsewhere
is that 'our past harmony is no guarantee of future security'[2]
and that Honolulu is now building up the ghetto geography,
authority, and mentality which may break forth twenty

---

[1] Rev. Charles T. Crane, 'It Can't Happen Here – Or Can It?', *Honolulu Star-Bulletin* (31 January 1968).
[2] Ibid.

years hence in the racial violence which plagues the large cities of continental United States. Another prominent Honolulu clergyman and newspaper columnist has voiced a somewhat similar concern—'the very real possibility that as our society changes, much of what we have enjoyed may be threatened by an increase in racial tensions', basing his fears upon the increase in the proportion of Caucasians and the possible increase in the number of Negroes in the population.[3]

A Mainland journalist who prefers to come to Hawaii to write his books because he is 'less aware of racial tension here than elsewhere in the United States', speaks out nevertheless even more ominously of racial crises which he claims are near at hand. He insists that 'Hawaii is becoming race conscious, reflecting Mainland prejudices', and he 'foresees the day when the racial tensions which tear Mainland cities will envelope Honolulu'.

The whole tourist-based philosophy is fallacious. It's phony. Hawaii is politically disappointing. The State which represents the only true ethnic melting pot in the nation ought to be leading in the debate over our racial crisis. Leadership ought to be taken on a State level. Instead, the Mainland sets the pace and the people of Hawaii tag along. . . . Hawaii, committed to a phony policy of tourism cannot escape consequences of the mistakes it is making.[4]

To conclude as these observers do that Hawaii will experience similar racial disturbances to those in the large metropolitan centres of continental United States because the Islands share some of the same conditions of rapid social change is, of course, the result of questionable logic, and there is little empirical evidence to support such predictions.

Probably the psychological basis of some of these dire forecasts is a reaction to what appears frequently as an official attitude of a strong complacency with respect to race relations in Hawaii. The newcomer to the Islands, if he is

[3] Rev. Larry Jones, 'Racial Strife Could Hit Here', *Honolulu Advertiser* (28 January 1968).
[4] Interview with Paul Jacobs in *Honolulu Advertiser* (28 December 1967).

not immediately captured by the enthusiasm for the liberality in race relations which he encounters, and especially if
any of his initial contacts in the community prove unplea-
sant, may readily focus his irritations upon the exaggerated
claims of a unique inter-racial Utopia. The bitterness with
which an occasional visitor protests against the alleged
'myth of interracial concord that imbues Hawaii with a bliss-
ful but false glow of human harmony' grows in part from its
appearing to have been 'foisted on the rest of the world . . . so
pompously and self-righteously as to induce a sort of mental
nausea'.[5]

It is perhaps not surprising that the pride and satisfaction
which residents of Hawaii unquestionably derive from the
absence in their community of the extreme racial tensions
found in many other parts of the world, especially when this
fact is constantly re-emphasized by every visiting celebrity,
should sometimes appear to critics as insufferable arrogance.
This ethnocentric pride seems nothing short of pharasaical
hypocrisy when Island enthusiasts—usually recent arrivals—
have on a few occasions in recent years presumed to instruct
the 'less fortunate peoples elsewhere' on how to order their
race relations according to the Hawaiian model.

No experienced observer of the Island scene can fail to
recognize that Hawaiian race relations are the product of
those forces—some of them assuredly shared with other
regions—which have operated within the peculiar historical
and geographic circumstances in Hawaii and that Hawaii
holds no magical formula for exorcizing the evil spirits of
racial discord and distrust in other parts of the world.
No unique principle of natural selection has operated in
Hawaii to breed a people without prejudices or resentments
towards those who surpass them in the competition for
status and the material comforts of life. Nor is there reason
for believing that a benign climate can absorb the truculence,
pettiness, and selfishness in men's dispositions any more in
these Islands than elsewhere in the world.

[5] 'Letter to the Editor' by an American grantee at the East-West Center of
Cultural Interchange at the University of Hawaii, *Honolulu Advertiser* (16
September 1967).

Indeed, the very rapidity with which old barriers to social intercourse and egalitarian relations across racial lines have broken down within the present generation has contributed to the emergence of what many observers assume to be an unprecedented outbreak of racial prejudice. Especially within the period following the granting of statehood to Hawaii, there have been, both in public as well as in private, increasing expressions of concern about supposed manifestations of racial prejudice. Although objective indices of the prevalence of such charges are difficult to establish, there is evidence, especially in the press and through other mass media, of a greater disposition to take account of the possible existence of racialism. For example, a series of editorials and feature articles appeared in both of the two principal newspapers during 1967 and 1968 citing evidence of the presence or absence of 'race prejudice in Hawaii'. One such series early in 1968 consisted of an analysis of the points of view presented during two days of an 'all talk' radio station in which the majority of the callers appeared to be Caucasian 'racists [airing] their hates', particularly towards Negroes.

A number of the newspaper editorials on race relations during this period were devoted to defending the Islands from the charges of prejudice, although in some instances the major emphasis was rather on the efforts of the press to bring evidence of discrimination and prejudice to public attention.

. . . this is not a land of lotus eaters but of people who are both individuals and members of racial groups who sometimes distrust and discriminate against each other . . . the press is accused of either not mentioning or covering up the racial situation here. We can only cite some examples to the contrary. Most recently was a three-part series on race relations by an Advertiser reporter which began: 'Hawaii has subtle racial discrimination in housing, in business, in religion and in relationships with the Armed Forces, according to members of all ethnic groups recently surveyed by the Advertiser. But economic pressure is breaking down the barriers in housing and in business, most of the participants in the survey agreed.' . . . The Pacific Club's ban on Oriental members and Governor Burns' refusal to join because of that was the subject of stories and comments. So were old racial barriers in the plush housing of Kahala.

The essential point about Hawaii is that it is a community of minorities in varying degrees from old elements of segregation, to forms of peaceful coexistence, to broader forms of integration. The thing that has won Hawaii praise around the world is neither perfection nor propaganda exaggerating the harmony. It is that here varying groups of people have managed to both prosper and grow closer together in a Polynesian-American environment. The result is a racial situation that is one of the best in the world.[6]

The increasing disposition to concede that the millennium in race relations has not yet arrived in Hawaii and that behind the façade of perfection sometimes presented by public figures and advertising agents there are ordinary people with ordinary weaknesses and foibles is unquestionably one of the more significant advances towards greater realism in human relations which have been brought about in the period since Statehood. This reduction in the pretensions of inter-racial perfection should also help to eliminate the present danger that Hawaii might be called upon to validate its claims and to produce the magical formula.

What is perhaps not so commonly recognized is that the more frequent overt expressions of inter-racial disaffection and resentments in recent years do not necessarily represent any deterioration in the basic nature of race relations. The fact that greater public attention is now directed to the violations of Hawaii's racial code and that greater resentment is expressed towards the gaps between profession and practice reflects rather an increased sensitivity to the claims which human beings as such may rightfully impose upon each other. The inequities in the treatment of individuals on the basis of race which a generation ago were simply taken for granted by the immigrant generation as one of the inevitabilities of a plantation frontier or were borne in restrained silence by their children in a still-stratified social system have no longer been accepted as natural and

[6] 'Our Race Relations', *Honolulu Advertiser* (16 September 1967).

inevitable. What some observers interpret as a rising belligerency and resentfulness on the part of Islanders is in fact a more open and honest expression of feelings which an earlier state of affairs kept under cover. Most of the increasing numbers of newly arrived Mainland Haoles, who find themselves for the first time in the role of a racial minority in Hawaii, are, as noted above, even less at a loss to object openly and vigorously to any real or implied violation of their personal rights.

As sociologists are fond of pointing out, prejudice is frequently a protective device developed by groups whose vested interests or goals are either threatened or resisted by other groups, and it emerges most prominently, therefore, under conditions of rapid social change as individuals or groups move out of their accustomed places. Thus prejudice, as the overt expression of uncritical sentiments of derogation or hostility towards other groups, was unquestionably least evident in Hawaii during the period of plantation dominance when racial distinctions were marked but also most commonly taken for granted as a natural and essential part of the established order. On the other hand, it has been during the period since World War II when the barriers to equal opportunity across ethnic lines have been most rapidly falling, and especially during the decade following Statehood with its additional transformations, that many Islanders have become most acutely aware of racial tensions. One might say that in Hawaii, as well as in other areas of racial contacts, prejudice is part of the price that must be paid for desired change.

One of the post-war and post-Statehood developments which some observers would interpret as an expression of prejudice but which might equally well be regarded as a form of progress is the resurgence of interest in the ancestral cultures of the several immigrant groups and even among the native Hawaiians. Throughout the period of American political domination in Hawaii, a central objective of administrative agencies and the official moulders of public opinion has been the assimilation or, more specifically, the Americanization of the numerous diverse ethnic groups in the population. The public schools and the American press, for example, joined forces during the first four decades of the present century in waging war on the foreign-language schools and press which had developed among the various immigrant groups. These and the numerous mutual-aid organizations, particularly in the Chinese, Japanese, Korean, and Filipino communities, were looked upon with considerable suspicion as serious threats to the success of the 'melting-pot' theory which had unquestioned acceptance in official circles. Even in the post-war period, when this theory has been called into serious question nationally on grounds of both feasibility and desirability, the disposition has persisted locally of equating Hawaii's tradition of race relations with the elimination of any observable ethnic differences, and the 'melting-pot' is still frequently extolled, even though the concept has never been an especially appropriate one since people do not melt.

As a consequence of the rising educational and economic status of all the ethnic groups in Hawaii since World War II and the diminishing differences in average positions among them, the need for conformity in all other respects has come to appear less urgent than it once was. Once having established themselves on the basis of criteria most highly accepted in the wider community, the descendants of the immigrant groups could afford to take account of those sources of distinction that were peculiarly their own. The renewed interest of third and fourth generation Chinese, for example, in the mutual-aid societies established by the immigrant generation is undoubtedly stimulated in part by their desire to share in the inflated economic value of the property belonging to these organizations, but there is also present a mounting pride in the history and cultural achievements of their ancestors. So also the Hawaiian-born citizens of Japanese ancestry who participate in such traditional institutions as the *kumi* and the *tanamoshi* (primary-group organizations for mutual assistance and credit) or the sects of Japanese Buddhism may derive some material benefits from their associations, but the psychological returns on an additional basis of group and self-respect may be even more important.

H

The consciousness of being contributors to the cultural wealth of Hawaii by transmitting the gifts derived from their ancestral past need not result in prejudicial attitudes towards all others, nor has the situation in Hawaii since World War II provided any significant basis for a fear that this was taking place. Rather, the limited revival of traditional cultures which has occurred in conjunction with ethnic celebrations such as the Chinese New Year and Ching-Ming, the Japanese Hana Matsuri and Bon festivals, or the Filipino Rizal Day serve to enrich the life of the entire community, and even the tourist-inspired Chinese Narcissus Festival, the Japanese Cherry Blossom Festival, and Aloha Week provide a significant residue of cross-cultural appreciation and understanding. A growing recognition by the major newspapers of the positive community values which may inhere in Hawaii's polycultural heritage has somewhat belatedly supplanted an earlier constant and exclusive stress upon the theme of assimilation and Americanization.

The role in Hawaii of racially-oriented clubs and societies has always been a proper and serious question of public concern. . . . Prior to World War II and prior to Statehood there were serious questions whether the societies were preventing the assimilation of our people of various races and cultures into a truly homogeneous American community. . . . We are deep in their debt for the succession of cultural festivals we enjoy through the year and for the points of contact they lend for visitors. In this they give the Hawaiian community a cultural richness that no other state enjoys. And it is in this area that Hawaii's need for an appreciation of its cultural societies is increasing, not diminishing. . . . The preservation here of respect for our various parent cultures, and of understanding for them may help to contribute to the great work that needs to be done in the years ahead in the Pacific in terms of helping nations to work together to achieve the new wealth, the new opportunities that really are possible.[7]

The renewed interest in such culturally oriented societies and movements emanating from Hawaii's several ethnic heritages, should not, however, be confused with the survival of those racially exclusive organizations which arose in an earlier day when social status was so closely associated with

[7] 'A Richness of Cultures', *Honolulu Star-Bulletin* (27 January 1968).

race. The most notable, although not the only, instances of this latter trend, naturally enough, have been and still are to be found within the Haole community. Having enjoyed the privileged positions—in terms of wealth, power, and social prestige on the plantation and political frontiers of Hawaii—from which the immigrant groups were automatically excluded, the Haoles of an earlier generation lived in a social world somewhat apart from those less fortunate than themselves and the social structures and associations which reflected and guaranteed this differential status came into being. A variety of clubs, lodges, fraternal organizations, and particularly the associations centred around the privileges of leisure and wealth were at the same time symbols of racial exclusiveness, and in the times of rapid social change since the Pacific war, they have also been in Hawaii as elsewhere the bastions of defence against the possible assaults upon what were interpreted to be vested racial rights.

However, in the face of an increasingly critical attitude towards such racial exclusiveness, one after the other of the Haole-controlled associations have found it expedient to drop whatever racial restrictions they may once have imposed. As early as 1926 with the extension of the Lions' Club movement to Hawaii, the interracial Honolulu branch of this Mainland organization put pressure on the national organization to drop its constitutional restriction of membership to whites only. Rotary International, with its greater prestige at an earlier date in Hawaii's history, was also tardier in opening its ranks to non-Caucasians, but it also had begun to admit eminent persons of Oriental and Hawaiian ancestry well before World War II. Until the late 1960s the influential Pacific Club, which dates back to the middle of the last century, resisted the pressures of public opinion by refusing to admit non-Caucasians as members, although a token representation of Part-Hawaiians had previously been allowed to join. In 1969 there were still several leisure time and fraternal organizations with highly desirable recreational facilities which denied membership to persons of Oriental ancestry.

RACIAL GHETTOS AND RESIDENTIAL INTEGRATION

Far more critical to the social well-being of any community than the ability of all persons regardless of their racial or ethnic origins to gain access to desired voluntary organizations is their opportunity to obtain satisfactory living accommodations. In this respect, also, Hawaii has undergone significant changes during the present century, although many of these shifts had occurred prior to the war in the Pacific.

As a necessary part of their paternalistic labour policy, the plantations had to provide housing for their workers; also a system of separate racial settlements or 'camps' was universally employed because it was most satisfactory to the workers and provided the best means of labour control. This arrangement enabled the immigrants, in their encounter with a strange and frequently hostile environment, to derive some comfort and consolation from the presence of others speaking the same language and observing familiar customs and traditions. Within these racial camps or rural ghettos, it was possible to maintain some semblance of the familiar modes of life of the homeland, even in spite of dreary barracks type of housing and a predominantly adult male population. Perhaps the principal present-day survivals of this segregative policy are the ethnic names, for example, 'Spanish', 'Korean', 'Filipino', still attached to a neighbourhood or 'Camp', which was first inhabited exclusively by persons of a particular ethnic group, even though no one of that background resides in the area any longer.

So, also, as plantation workers and their families gravitated to the cities and towns in search of better economic opportunities, they first sought out neighbourhoods where members of their own ethnic group were already in residence. Because of their relatively low economic status the migrants to the cities could only afford to pay the rentals in the deteriorating slum sections where residence was giving way to industry. Thus, as a consequence of the economic forces operating on the immigrants and their desire for the personal warmth and comfort derived from the immediate presence of their countrymen and the familiar associations of the homeland, the racial ghettos of Honolulu and the other urban centres of Hawaii were brought into being.

These little ethnic enclaves within the city 'zones of transition'—Chinatowns, Japanese camps, Portuguese settlements, and modified Filipino *barrios*, each with its characteristic institutions and modes of life—obviously constituted segregated ghettos. But in a strict sociological sense they were quite comparable to the separate and culturally self-sufficient communities which every immigrant community seeks to establish for itself in an alien or potentially hostile environment: Americans in Bangkok, Australians in Port Moresby, the British in Calcutta, the French in Saigon—their quarters differed fundamentally from the immigrant ghettos in Honolulu, Chicago, New York, or London in that they were situated in the economically select areas of the city and provided the choicest facilities of their respective cultures.

As recently as 1930, there were some twenty-five distinct Japanese 'camps' in the city of Honolulu within which the immigrants and their children could partially duplicate the cultural atmosphere of a Japanese village with its characteristic facilities of Buddhist temples, and Shinto shrines, teahouses, language schools, bath-houses, and places for *sumo* and *judo*. Chinatown was still the centre of the more important old-world societies and the residence of more than a quarter of the entire Chinese population of Honolulu. By this time, however, their rise in economic status and their further assimilation into Island society had enabled and encouraged the other three-quarters to establish themselves outside of Chinatown. Two clearly marked areas of Portuguese settlement in Honolulu were evident in the census returns of 1920 and even the smaller ethnic groups in Honolulu, including Filipinos, Koreans, Puerto Ricans, Negroes, and Samoans, have shown the identical tendency to seek the comfort and security of neighbours of the same ethnic background, especially during the early period of their adjustment to the city.

Contrary to the widespread assumptions in continental United States that the racial ghetto is necessarily identified with human degradation and repression, under the conditions which have prevailed in Hawaii these colonies of a single ethnic group have served as a useful initial stage in a process of more complete integration within the larger community. Studies conducted in Honolulu in the late 1920s indicated that both the immigrants and their children residing in such ethnically segregated areas were less subject to the traumas of urban life than their contemporaries who lived in the contiguous slums outside the racial ghetto,[8] confirming R. E. Park's proposition that 'it is the immigrants who have maintained in this country their simple village religions and mutual aid organizations who have been most able to withstand the shock of the new environment'.[9] The fact that people know and gossip about one another within a common set of moral expectations and that they also feel obligated to support one another in times of crises, gives to the life of the ghetto resident a firmness of direction and stability that is scarcely possible elsewhere in the impersonal urban setting.

It has been the unfortunate experience of the racially identifiable immigrant groups, especially those marked by ineradicable physiological traits, that in most parts of the world they have been greatly restricted in their ability to move out of the ghetto: that legal and psychological walls have prevented their access to the greater opportunities outside. The circumstances of life in Hawaii, on the other hand, have tended to break down these racial barriers from the outside at a fairly rapid rate, particularly within the middle third of the twentieth century. The residential ghettos of Hawaii have served, rather, as the temporary stepping-stones for all the immigrant ethnic groups on their way to places of greater privilege and promise. In the case of the early immigrant arrivals in the city, the initial 'escape' from the ghetto was simply a move to another area of racial concentration offering better housing accommodations.

[8] A. W. Lind, 'The Ghetto and the Slums', *Social Forces* (IX, no. 2, December 1930), pp. 206–15.

[9] R. E. Park, E. W. Burgess, and R. D. McKenzie, *The City* (Chicago, University of Chicago Press, 1925), pp. 121–2.

Such, for example, was the movement from Honolulu's Chinatown during the 1920s to an area known as 'Chinese Hollywood', a then newly developed lower middle-class residential area in which the population became more than 80 per cent Chinese in a relatively short time. Chinese Hollywood, however, did not remain Chinese for very long, as the more ambitious and affluent moved on to still better residential areas further removed from Chinatown. In the meantime the Chinatown area was becoming more and more cosmopolitan in character, so much so that as early as 1920 there were as many Japanese in the district as Chinese, in addition to considerable numbers of Hawaiians, Part-Hawaiians, Filipinos, Portuguese, and other Caucasians. By 1960, less than a quarter of the residents in Chinatown were Chinese and this remnant of the earlier colony consisted chiefly of aged single males, living out their remaining years in the guild halls or above the stores maintained by the Chinese community in the district. The remaining three-quarters of the population were a pot-pourri of virtually all the many ethnic types in Hawaii, with single Filipino males forming somewhat more than a third of the total. A somewhat similar transformation, i.e., from an overwhelmingly mono-ethnic population to one that was racially cosmopolitan, occurred at a somewhat later date in Chinese Hollywood, and this indeed has been the dominant pattern of residential change especially in the post-war period in Honolulu and throughout the island of Oahu.

Of the various segregated ethnic communities, those dominated by Caucasians were unquestionably most resistant to erosion by the assimilative and secularizing processes of the city. For many years Manoa Valley, Upper Nuuanu Valley, Black Point, Alewa, Pacific, Makiki, and Maunalani Heights, and Kahala had been the high prestige areas of large well-kept gardens and expensive homes, owned and inhabited exclusively by Haoles. The higher economic positions and political power of the Haoles during the nineteenth and early twentieth centuries enabled them to secure the more desirable areas on the heights, in the more attractive valleys, and along the seashore; and once settled in these areas, the Haoles looked with disfavour on any invasion by outsiders. Informal agreements, if not regularized covenants, not to sell to non-Caucasians were definitely operative in some of these areas in the period prior to World War II when families of Oriental ancestry, in particular, were beginning to aspire to homes in these select areas.

The Japanese attack on Pearl Harbor in December 1941 occasioned the first major breach in the Haole ghetto walls, as many of the residents sought to evacuate to the Mainland and were willing to dispose of their property to anyone who would buy. This was the opening wedge for an extensive invasion of the Haole strongholds by non-Caucasians, which seemed to portend to some of the Haoles who remained the inevitable deterioration of the district and collapse of land values. Actually, of course, land values have mounted steadily as an increasing number of potential purchasers other than Haoles have been able to enter the market. With the phenomenal growth of the city since the war, other areas of exclusive Haole residence have developed, especially in the areas devoted to military housing and tourist accommodations, but their racial homogeneity has invariably been short-lived.

It is not to be assumed that all the various ethnic groups are distributed residentially in proportion to their numbers in the total population. Just as in the rural portions of the Islands, owing to historical circumstances, the plantations have continued to draw their workers somewhat disproportionately from among the Filipinos and Japanese, so also within the cities most neighbourhoods are overweighted with the population of one or more of the various ethnic groups. It is possible, for example, to designate areas of Honolulu where each of the five largest ethnic groups—Japanese, Caucasian, Hawaiian, Chinese, and Filipinos, in that order[10]—is more heavily represented than any

[10] The percentage distribution of these groups in the total population of Honolulu in 1960 was as follows: Japanese, 37·1 per cent; Caucasian, 27·3 per cent; Hawaiian, 15·1 per cent; Chinese, 10·2 per cent; and Filipino, 7·4 per cent.

other, or than might be expected on the basis of their total population. However, all five of these groups had some residents in all but one[11] of the seventy-two census tracts in 1960. Even the extremely small Negro population, constituting only 0·4 per cent of the total population of Honolulu in 1960, was spread residentially over all but ten of the seventy-two tracts. Certainly there is no Negro ghetto in Hawaii, where rental units are so very limited, although as the last arrivals in the community and the least known among the residents, Negroes have sometimes met difficulties in obtaining satisfactory housing.

The experience of what was prior to 1941 an upper middle-class and exclusively Haole residential area in Manoa Valley reflects the type of racial integration in housing which has occurred throughout the Islands during the post-war period. Of eighteen homes on or adjacent to a small street in the middle of the valley, of which sixteen were occupied by Haoles and two by racially mixed families in professional or proprietary pursuits prior to the war, the owners and occupants twenty-seven years later were ethnically distributed as follows: five of Japanese ancestry, five Haoles, two Portuguese, one Chinese, one Filipino, and four racially mixed. The middle-class character of the neighbourhood has remained approximately the same and property values have increased by 300 to 500 per cent. Ever since the war, throughout the Islands the long-term trend in housing has clearly been towards a further decline in the need or desire for ethnic concentrations and towards the emergence of a community in which the desirability of a neighbourhood is determined not by considerations of race but rather by those of economic costs and class, social status, and physical convenience and attractiveness.

THE NEGRO: A RECENT TEST CASE

Still another area of post-war development in Hawaii's relations which deserves some attention, if only because of the queries from Mainland visitors, relates to the role of the Negro. Chiefly because of the prominent and essentially

[11] This was a purely military community.

tragic part which the Negro problem has occupied in the American experience in continental United States during the 1960s, one of the first questions raised by visitors is 'What about the Negro in Hawaii?' Even the Island press has felt compelled to raise such hypothetical questions as 'Would aloha survive if 100,000 Negroes with little education and only the most minimal of marketable skills were deposited on our island tomorrow?'[12]

Numerically, the Negro has never constituted more than a minute part of Hawaii's population, and the latest census, with the largest number ever recorded, returned a figure of less than 5,000 or 0·8 per cent of the total population. Of these, fully half were members of the armed forces and even less permanently established in the community than the small civilian group. There had been persons living in Hawaii from the early part of the nineteenth century who in continental United States would have been classified in the census as Negroes and accorded a corresponding social status in the community. Under the conditions which prevailed in Hawaii prior to annexation by the United States, however, such persons were sometimes referred to by the natives as '*haole eleele*', or black foreigners, but were not separately identified from other foreigners in the census, and were able to achieve positions of distinction within the community commensurate with their individual abilities.

The introduction of the census category of Negro in 1900 was required by policies established in continental United States, and apart from that requirement there probably would not have been any separate enumeration of Negroes until after World War II, since less than 700 were reported in each census prior to 1950. The two world wars brought large numbers of the armed forces, both white and coloured, to Hawaii, and particularly during World War II it was feared that both the discriminatory practices and the prejudicial attitudes towards Negroes which characterized military installations on the Mainland might be transferred to the Island situation. To avoid the possibility of friction, it even seemed necessary to compromise the Island code of

[12] *Honolulu Star-Bulletin* (21 November 1967).

race relations by setting up a separate system of community recreational facilities to accommodate those members of the military whose prejudices would not permit them to associate amicably with Negroes and the dark-complexioned troops of the Islands, and some local tradesmen such as barbers and hotel and restaurant operators yielded to threats of boycott by Mainland troops if they continued to serve Negroes. Fortunately most, although not all, of those practices and the associated attitudes disappeared at the end of the war, with removal of the instigating forces.

The post-war period has not witnessed any large-scale influx of Negroes seeking relief from the depressed conditions in the rural South or the ghettos of northern cities of the Mainland, and of the small number who have migrated to Hawaii, a disproportionate number, as compared with the Mainland, have been able to establish themselves in preferred occupations. As one of the last ethnic groups to emerge into consciousness within the Hawaiian setting, the Negroes have been viewed by other Islanders with the uncertainty bordering on mistrust which has been invariably the experience of the newcomer to the community, and especially on Oahu where desirable housing is at such a premium and where over 90 per cent of the Negroes are concentrated. This is an area in which the newcomer is most likely to find himself at a disadvantage. Apart from the sizeable group of Negroes in the military service and residing at the various military installations, there has been no tendency towards the formation of a separate Negro ghetto in Honolulu. Although the Smith Street area in downtown Honolulu has been commonly associated in the popular mind with the Negro, and although certain institutions have emerged there which cater especially to the Negro service men on leave, only a handful of Negroes actually live there.

Unlike the immigrant labour groups which experienced from the outset an occupational and economic segregation at the bottom levels of the social scale, the Negroes have been able to enter the Island social structure at different levels depending in large part upon their previous experience and attainments. As a consequence there has never been among them the cohesive dispositions either to form a separate community or to organize the mutual-aid or protective agencies which have figured so prominently in the experience of most of the other ethnic groups in Hawaii.

Even the one organization which has emerged among the Negroes, a branch of the National Association for the Advancement of Colored People, has had a distinctly spotty career. An attempt to establish a Chapter of the N.A.A.C.P. during World War II by recently arrived Mainland defence workers was vigorously opposed by Island residents of Negro background who contended that there was no need for such an organization in Hawaii and that it would merely serve to create tensions where there had been none. Although the recent arrivals were able to prevail, the Chapter was short-lived and it was not until the early 1960s that the organization again came into existence in Hawaii, largely because of the interest generated by the problems of the Negro on the U.S. Mainland. Some attention has been directed in the succeeding years to matters of Negro adjustment in Hawaii, but it has been the concern over the tensions on the continent, heightened from time to time by visits from celebrated figures in the Mainland struggle, such as Martin Luther King and Dick Gregory, which has really sustained the organization. A number of different ventures with Christian churches around a Negro constituency have been successful for only relatively short periods of time. The general tendency among Negroes who have settled permanently in Hawaii has been to identify themselves with the wider clubs and organizations in the community and thus the general public ceases to conceive of them as Negroes.

THE ULTIMATE TEST

In the final analysis, what matters most in race relations is not what people may say about each other or even what may happen on an inter-racial basis to any small segment of the population, but rather how people in general deal with each other across racial lines. There is, of course, no simple and completely adequate index of so complex an aspect of human experience. It has been argued, however, that the choices people make with respect to their companions in the most intimate of human relationships—marriage —afford at least a significant clue of their regard for the ethnic groups of which these individuals are a part.

Hawaii's claims to distinction can be questioned in many of the areas for which supporters have been prone to give it credit, or critics have levelled blame—for both the profession and the corresponding practice of racial equality, for the propagation of the aloha spirit, and for the encouragement of cross-cultural relations and inter-ethnic associations. Although the statistical data for most corresponding areas are unfortunately lacking, there can be little doubt that Hawaii's ratio of association in marriage and family building across sharply differentiated racial and cultural barriers is among the highest anywhere in the world. Hawaii, of course, shared with other colonial regions the extra-legal fusion of racial stocks which invariably occurs in frontier regions where the invaders, consisting chiefly of single men a long way from home and the traditional restraints, interbreed with the native population. What is distinctive about Hawaii in this respect is that under the conditions prevailing here pressure was exerted at an early stage to regularize and socially sanction cross-cultural unions and the families resulting therefrom.

For well over a century marriages between native Hawaiians and Haoles and between members of the immigrant groups and Haoles or Hawaiians have occurred with increasing frequency and, if not positively encouraged by the several ethnic groups, these marriages have been given sanction by law and commonly by a religious ceremony attended by both relatives and friends. During the past fifty years and more such has been the interest in this area of Hawaiian experience that detailed records have been kept of the ethnic background of both brides and grooms. Thus it has been possible to chart the directional trends and the extent of out-marriages among all the major ethnic groups.

Inter-racial marriage, of course, runs counter to the essen-

TABLE 7

INTER-RACIAL MARRIAGES AS PERCENTAGE OF ALL MARRIAGES, 1912–64

		1912–1916*	1920–1930*	1930–1940	1940–1949†	1950–1959‡	1960–1964‡
		% Out-marriages					
Hawaiian	Grooms	19·4	33·3	55·2	66·3	78·9	85·9
	Brides	39·9	52·1	62·7	77·2	81·5	85·4
Part-Hawaiian	Grooms	52·1	38·8	41·0	36·9	41·3	47·0
	Brides	66·2	57·7	57·9	64·2	58·4	56·8
Caucasian	Grooms	17·3	24·3	22·4	33·8	37·4	35·1
	Brides	11·7	13·8	10·7	10·2	16·4	21·1
Chinese	Grooms	41·7	24·8	28·0	31·2	43·6	54·8
	Brides	5·7	15·7	28·5	38·0	45·2	56·6
Japanese	Grooms	0·5	2·7	4·3	4·3	8·7	15·7
	Brides	0·2	3·1	6·3	16·9	19·1	25·4
Korean	Grooms	26·4	17·6	23·5	49·0	70·3	77·1
	Brides	0·0	4·9	39·0	66·7	74·5	80·1
Filipino	Grooms	21·8	25·6	37·5	42·0	44·5	51·2
	Brides	2·8	1·0	4·0	21·0	35·8	47·5
Puerto Rican	Grooms	24·4	18·6	29·8	39·5	51·3	65·0
	Brides	26·4	39·7	42·8	50·3	60·5	67·2
Total		11·5	19·2	22·8	28·6	32·8	37·6

Source: Romanzo Adams, Interracial Marriage in Hawaii (New York, Macmillan Co., 1937), pp. 336–9; Annual Reports of the Bureau of Vital Statistics (Honolulu, 1943–9); Annual Reports, Department of Health Statistical Supplements (Honolulu, 1950–64).

* Derived from Romanzo Adams, Interracial Marriage in Hawaii, pp. 336–9.
† Bureau of Vital Statistics, 1 July 1940–30 June 1948 and calendar year 1949.
‡ Bureau of Health Statistics, calendar years 1950–64.

tial nature of any viable racial group; as long as it retains a consciousness of possessing values and traditions separate and distinct from all others, pressure will inevitably be exerted to discourage members from marrying outside the group. The restraining influence of the transplanted racial group on its members tends to diminish, however, with the length of residence in the new environment with its diversity in standards and values, and the rates of out-marriage are likely to rise.

Data in Table 7 reveal a fairly high ratio of out-marriage for the entire population, of 11·5 per cent, even at the beginning of the fifty-year period, but this percentage mounted steadily in the subsequent periods to 19·2 per cent in the 1920s, 22·8 per cent in the 1930s, 28·6 per cent in the 1940s, 32·8 per cent in the 1950s, and reaching an unprecedented level of 37·6 per cent during the first five years of the 1960s. The expectation in some quarters that the influx of Caucasians to the Islands following Statehood would bring a significant reduction in the ratio of out-marriages, or even a reversal in the upward trend, has obviously not been borne out.

Several demographic factors have modified to some degree the mounting tendency towards out-marriage, but have in no instance permanently reversed the trend. For example, the extremely high disproportion of males among the immigrant Chinese and Koreans induced an abnormally high out-marriage rate at an early period of the group's experience in Hawaii, which declined temporarily as the sex ratio within the group became more nearly normal. For most of the immigrant men in such groups, if they were to marry at all in the new setting, it had to be with women of another ethnic group, and the extremely low rate of out-marriage of females at that period testifies to the high premium at which they were held by men of their own group. After the temporary decline in the out-marriage of Chinese and Korean males during the 1920s, the trend for both males and females has swung sharply upwards.

The relatively small number of available marriage mates of either sex among the Koreans and the Puerto Ricans, and in later years among the pure Hawaiians, has contributed to the very high out-marriage rates among them, whereas the large number of persons of Japanese ancestry in both sexes has encouraged marriage within the group.

A further analysis of the race of both brides and grooms involved in the out-marriages over the first five years of the 1960s reveals a wide catholicity in the choices, with all but one of the possible sixty-four combinations of ethnic groups, large and small, represented. There is evidence of a somewhat greater selectivity in the choice of out-group marriage mates, especially among men of ethnic groups with strong and highly formalized family traditions, such as the Chinese and Japanese and even the Caucasians. The Hawaiians, on the other hand, have been much less discriminating in their marriage choices, bestowing their favours quite freely on those in other ethnic groups who sought them.

Not surprisingly, religion has played a prominent, although statistically undeterminable and probably declining, role in the determination of out-marriage choices among the various ethnic groups over the past half century. In his study of the records of inter-ethnic marriage between 1912 and 1934, Romanzo Adams discovered that a common Roman Catholic affiliation was associated with and seemed to explain partially the greater disposition of Filipinos, Spanish, Puerto Ricans, and Portuguese to find marriage mates across the strikingly different racial lines they represent rather than from among members of other more racially congruous groups.[13] On the other hand, he noted a high disposition towards in-marriage among the ethnic groups for whom the family and its values had become the central focus of religious veneration. In the absence of counteracting forces, such as the demographic factors mentioned above, or the cross-cultural influence of a Catholic Church, all the immigrant peasant groups from both Europe and Asia gave evidence of a tendency to find marriage mates within their own ethnic group.[14] Traditional religious pres-

[13] Romanzo Adams, *Interracial Marriage in Hawaii* (New York, Macmillan Co., 1938), pp. 138, 180.
[14] Ibid., p. 198.

sures of a similar nature have continued down to the present, although their impact upon the rates of inter-ethnic and intra-ethnic marriages is much less pronounced now than it was a generation ago, and one may expect a further decline in this influence as life in the community becomes even more secularized.[15]

Doubts inevitably arise as to whether marriages across racial lines can possibly be as enduring as those within the separate ethnic groups, the usual assumption being that the more deeply rooted differences in customs and values inherent in marriages across ethnic lines necessarily entail greater hazards than marriages within the group. Evidence gathered by Romanzo Adams in 1927 seemed to confirm this impression, indicating that the ratio of divorced persons was significantly lower among the in-married of all races than among the out-married and that 'divorce rates were highest among . . . the members of the racial groups that outmarry the most'.[16] Considering the relatively early stage in the assimilative process, this situation was quite normal at that time.

Thirty years later, following a generation of public school and community contacts, however, it appeared that although the family stability, judged by the absence of divorce, was still somewhat greater among in-married than among out-married couples, the difference had been greatly reduced in the intervening period, and that 'among five of Hawaii's nine major ethnic groups—all with divorce rates above the average—family breakdown was significantly less among those who had married out than among those who found marriage mates within their own ethnic group'.[17] Even among the Chinese and Japanese, whose overall divorce rates were the lowest of any of the major ethnic groups, 'out-

[15] As the proportion of persons of mixed racial ancestry increases in the population and the lines of demarcation between the groups become more and more indistinct, so also the terms inter-ethnic and intra-ethnic marriage become more obscure.

[16] Romanzo Adams, *Interracial Marriage in Hawaii* (New York, Macmillan Co., 1938), p. 225.

[17] Andrew W. Lind, 'Interracial Marriage as Affecting Divorce in Hawaii', *Sociology and Social Research* (no. 49, October 1964), p. 21.

I

TABLE 8

BIRTHS IN HAWAII BY RACE OF KNOWN PARENTS, 1960-4

Race of father	Haw'n	Part-Haw'n	Caucasian	Chinese	Japanese	Korean	Philipino	Puerto Rican	All others	Total	% Mixed
					Race of Mother						
Hawaiian	242	701	150	18	62	5	57	12	9	1,256	80·7
Part-Hawaiian	456	8,243	1,803	503	1,068	109	1,174	165	106	13,627	100·0
Caucasian	161	2,887	24,870	304	1,407	168	972	314	262	31,345	20·7
Chinese	23	475	223	2,128	694	49	106	13	13	3,724	42·9
Japanese	49	951	434	323	15,150	160	287	25	18	17,397	12·9
Korean	10	99	68	57	283	188	35	2	2	744	74·7
Filipino	162	2,167	656	130	582	49	6,521	181	202	10,650	38·8
Puerto Rican	35	393	174	16	63	7	126	584	10	1,371	60·0
All others	30	354	191	16	68	7	88	27	1,237	2,877	42·4
Total	1,167	18,246	28,569	3,495	19,377	742	9,366	1,287	2,718	82,991	39·2
% Mixed	78·8	100·0	12·9	39·1	21·8	74·7	30·4	57·4	54·5	39·2	

Source: Data derived from *Statistical Reports*, *Department of Health, State of Hawaii* (Honolulu, 1960-4).

marriages of men with women of the other group may result in fewer divorces than the in-marriage in either group'.[18]

The inevitable consequence of the mounting trends in mixed racial marriages and of their increasing stability is the appearance of a future generation of citizens of Hawaii who trace their ancestry to two or more of the remaining racial stocks. No set of impersonal statistics can do justice to the inter-cultural drama involved in that process, but at the same time there is perhaps no single set of facts which more adequately epitomizes the present and future race relations of the Islands than the table of the mixed racial ancestry of the children born in recent years.

Owing to the system of classification employed, an indeterminate proportion of the parents listed in Table 8 as being of mixed ancestry (except among the Hawaiians and Caucasians) are themselves of mixed ancestry, and hence well over 40 per cent of the births recorded during this period would be the descendants of two or more different racial stocks. All possible combinations of racial types have some representation in the table, and particularly among the part-Hawaiians, Chinese, Koreans, and Filipinos, several different racial strains may be included. In the light of the widespread assumption, still found even in some 'scientific' literature, that the Oriental races retain a pride of ancestry in which all other breeds are held unworthy of inclusion in the sacred family circle, the high proportion of out-marriages and of legitimate children of mixed racial ancestry credited to the Chinese, Koreans, and even the Japanese are especially to be noted.

Without making the necessary corrections for the various demographic factors mentioned above, deductions directly from the foregoing tables as to the nature and extent of racial preferences and avoidances in the post-war period cannot properly be made. That they do exist there is still a variety of evidence, but it is equally apparent that such likes and dislikes are not fixed and immutable but are subject to striking alteration and obliteration to correspond with changes in the social atmosphere in the community. With a mounting

[18] Lind, *op. cit.*, p. 23.

proportion of the population of mixed racial ancestry and fusing increasingly with those of unmixed ancestry, the indiscriminate acceptance or rejection of an entire ethnic group becomes a psychological impossibility. The time is rapidly approaching when the lines of differentiation between the traditional racial groups, especially the smaller ones, will have become so vague and indistinct as to make further compilation of statistics in these terms virtually absurd. The time has already come when even in the privacy among friends it is the height of poor taste to speak disparagingly of any of Hawaii's ethnic groups lest one or more of those present proves to be closely related to it by descent or marriage.

The psychological frame of mind of a growing proportion of Hawaii's population parallels, if it does not conform to, that of a University co-ed who in 1966 wrote of herself:

Just who should I tell you that I am. I come from many different racial lines. Two of my grandparents were immigrant laborers from Japan, one of whose sons most unfilially married the daughter of a Chinese coolie wedded to a Part-Hawaiian lass of God-only-knows-how-many sailor strains. According to your census enumerators I am Part-Hawaiian, and when I am with my Hawaiian kin-folk, I can dispose of as much fish and poi and dance the hula with the best of them. But I am half Japanese, and my father's relatives have succeeded pretty well in instilling some of the ancestral sense of decorum and love of the quiet beauty of Japan, at least when I am with them. (My Japanese grandparents resurrected their disowned and figuratively buried son when he presented them with their first grandchild.) With my Chinese relatives, I have participated actively and I hope reverently in the April Ching-ming celebrations at the cemetery and in the more boisterous festivals of the Chinese societies. My associations with Haoles and the American community have come not so much through relatives as from my contacts in high school and college, and although I glory in my Hawaiian, Japanese, and Chinese inheritance, I would have to confess that most of what really makes me what I am is the Americanisms I have unconsciously absorbed from living in this Hawaiian atmosphere.

Others would be far less enthusiastic about their own or

other's multicultural heritage, focusing rather on the gaps
which still remain between Hawaii's official professions of
racial equality and its actual practice in day-to-day experience. Few, however, of those who have been born and
nurtured in Hawaii in the generation prior to World War II
and have themselves experienced the changes wrought within that span of time would question the legitimacy and authenticity of such a point of view among the rising generation
in Hawaii. Whatever the uncertainties in the nature of
Hawaii's race relations in the future, and in a situation as
dynamic as that in the world of which Hawaii is a part,
change is one unquestioned certainty; another certainty is
that the blending of races within the increasingly large portion of the population cannot now or in the future be un-
scrambled.

Bibliography

ADAMS, ROMANZO. *The Education of the Boys of Hawaii and Their Economic Outlook* (Honolulu, University of Hawaii Research Publications, no. 4, January 1928).

—— *Interracial Marriage in Hawaii* (New York, Macmillan Co., 1938).

—— 'The Unorthodox Race Doctrine of Hawaii', E. B. Reuter (ed.), *Race and Culture Contacts* (New York, McGraw-Hill, 1934).

BAKER, RAY STANNARD. 'Wonderful Hawaii: A World Experiment Station', *The American Magazine* (no. 11, November 1911).

—— 'Wonderful Hawaii: A World Experiment Station', *The American Magazine* (no. 12, December 1911).

BARBER, JR., JOSEPH. *Hawaii: Restless Rampart* (New York, Bobbs-Merrill Co., 1940).

BEAGLEHOLE, ERNEST. *Some Modern Hawaiians* (Honolulu, University of Hawaii Press, 1937).

BURROWS, EDWIN G. *Hawaiian Americans* (Yale University Press, 1947).

COOK, JAMES. *A Voyage to the Pacific Ocean*, Vol. II (London, W. and H. Strahan, 1784).

FUCHS, LAWRENCE. *Hawaii Pono: A Social History* (New York, Harcourt, Brace and World, 1961).

HANDY, E. S. CRAIGHILL. *Cultural Revolution in Hawaii* (Honolulu, American Council, Institute of Pacific Relations, 1931).

HANDY, E. S. CRAIGHILL, EMORY, KENNETH P., AND OTHERS. *Ancient Hawaiian Civilization* (Rutland, Vermont, Charles E. Tuttle Co., 1965).

'Hawaii: Sugar-Coated Fort', *Fortune* (Vol. XXII, no. 2, August 1940).

HORMANN, BERNHARD. 'Native Welfare in Hawaii', *Proceedings of the Seventh Pacific Science Congress* (Auckland, 1953).

JUDD, LAURA FISH. *Honolulu: Sketches of the Life, Social, Political, and Religious, in the Hawaiian Islands from 1828 to 1861* (New York, Anson D. F. Randolph and Co., 1880).

KOLARZ, WALTER. 'The Melting Pot in the Pacific', *The Listener* (28 October 1954).

KUYKENDALL, RALPH. *The Hawaiian Kingdom, 1778–1854* (Honolulu, University of Hawaii, 1938).

LIND, ANDREW W. *Hawaii's Japanese* (Princeton, N.J., 1946).

—— *The Japanese in Hawaii Under War Conditions* (New York, Institute of Pacific Relations, 1943).

—— 'Some Modifications of Hawaiian Character', E. B. Reuter (ed.), *Race and Culture Contacts* (New York, McGraw-Hill, 1934).

PARK, ROBERT E. 'Our Racial Frontier on the Pacific', *Survey Graphic: East by West—Our Windows on the Pacific* (Vol. IX, no. 2, May 1926).

—— 'Race Relations and Certain Frontiers', E. B. Reuter (ed.), *Race and Culture Contacts* (New York, McGraw-Hill, 1934).

PARK, R. E., BURGESS, E. W., AND MCKENZIE, R. D. *The City* (Chicago, University of Chicago Press, 1925).

PORTEUS, STANLEY. *And Blow Not the Trumpet* (Palo Alto, Pacific Books, 1947).

REDFIELD, ROBERT. *The Primitive World and Its Transformations* (New York, Cornell University Press, 1953).

RICHARDSON, SETH W. *Law Enforcement in the Territory of Hawaii* (Washington, U.S. Printing Office, 1932).

THOMPSON, DAVID E. 'The ILWU as a Force for Interracial Unity in Hawaii', *Social Process in Hawaii* (no. 15, 1951).

WEINMAN, SAMUEL. *Hawaii: A Story of Imperialist Plunder* (New York, International Pamphlets, 1934).

WHITE, WILLIAM ALLEN. 'The Last of the Magic Isles', *Survey Graphic* (Vol. IX, no. 2, May 1926).

Index

Adams, Romanzo, 7–9, 16, 45, 59–60, 73, 114, 116, 117

Alii (chiefs), 71, 83

Aloha, spirit of: tourists and, 37–40, 67–8, 75, 77–8; typifies Hawaiians' attitude, 75–9, 82, 84, 85, 86, 110, 113

Aloha Week, 102

Americanization of Hawaii, 100–1, 102, 113

Americans in Hawaii; own plantations, 6, 18; early conflicts with Hawaiians, 23–4; included in 'other Caucasians' in the Census, 47–8; and Orientals' rivalry, 55–8; Hawaiian's imitation of, 81; and Hawaiians' hospitality, 74; and land, 88 (*see* United States)

Armed Forces, 4, 22, 26–9, 42, 49, 64, 110–11

Asiatic labour, 57–8

Assimilation in Hawaii, 95, 100, 102

Azores, immigrants from, 18

Baker, Roy Stannard, 5–6

Beaglehole, Ernest, 76

Big Five oligarchy, 20, 34

Bishop Museum, 76

Bishop, Princess Bernice Pauahi, 90, 91; B. P. Bishop Estate, 90–1

Black Power, and Hawaiian pride of ancestry, 94–5

Bon Festival, 102

Boston, missionaries from, 14

British, early conflicts with Hawaiians, 23–4

Buck, Sir Peter, 67

Buddhism, Japanese, 58, 101

Burns, Governor, 98

Burrows, Edwin G., 76

Canton, 44

Caucasians in Hawaii: and right to rule, 4; theory of racial superiority, 7; settle down with Hawaiians on equal terms, 8; introduce trading, 14; become citizens, 25; number of, 35, 47, 96; on sugar plantations, 45; as defined in the census, 46, 48, 49; and jobs, 61–2; incomes of, 63, 65; arrival in Hawaii, 68; opinion of Hawaiians, 69, 73–4; and land, 88; and racism, 98; in mixed marriages, 113–19 (*see* *Haoles*: 'Other Caucasians')

Census, 21, 46, 48–50, 61–2, 110

Chamber of Commerce, 77–8; Japanese, 95

Cherry Blossom Festival, 102

Children: of missionaries, 15; of foreigners, 48; poor school record of Hawaiian, 84–5; upbringing of Hawaiian, 86; of mixed marriages, 118–19

Chinese in Hawaii: as plantation labourers, 18, 21, 44–5; as defined in census, 21, 43, 44, 48; not citizens, 25; number of, 47; incomes of, 52–3, 63–5; jobs for, 54–6, 60–2; societies among, 95, 101, 120; ancestral culture of, 101–2; in mixed marriages, 114–15, 118–20; divorce among, 117

Chinese Hollywood, 107